D1522880

GLOBAL SENSE can help you...

- **TRIUMPH** over fear, anger and despair by claiming your personal power to change the world by changing yourself.

- **SEE** how our natural global interactivity makes us powerful since everything we think, say and do affects all life on earth.

- **CHOOSE** smart options in daily life that can help end war, restore our lost freedoms and heal our wounded planet.

- **CHALLENGE** the hidden emotional and mental habits that drive us to give up our liberty for the illusion of security.

- **EXPLORE** why brave men are liberating themselves from ancient cravings to dominate women and rule the world.

- **DISCOVER** a bold vision of democracy in *direct republics* that can forever change how we think about government.

- **LEARN** how progressives and libertarians can join forces to protect our natural rights and build peace through prosperity.

- **UNITE** spiritual growth and community politics to become an aware and effective global citizen in the 21st century.

Features an Inspiring Study Guide

"The American Revolution came about because independent voices like Thomas Paine rallied the people to independence.... We need to get back the revolutionary spirit of dissent and courage that brought us into existence in the first place."
  – BILL MOYERS on *Democracy Now*

"*Global Sense* is an awesome work that's urgently needed for our times. This is the type of book you read and then want to buy for your friends, relatives and neighbors.... *Global Sense* is the best personal growth book of the year."

    – COLORADO INDEPENDENT PUBLISHERS ASSN. EVVY AWARD

"Judah Freed has revisited Thomas Paine's *Common Sense* for the reawakening of democracy. *Global Sense* is about personal and social transformation, starting with the inner self feeling a genuine recognition of our rights and responsibilities. The book is a declaration of global interdependence."

    – VANDANA SHIVA, author, *Stolen Harvest* and *Earth Democracy*

"Judah Freed's update of the Thomas Paine classic is perfect for our tumultuous times, showing how these principles, first published in 1776, remain relevant in the 21st Century."

    – HOWARD ROTHMAN, author, *Companies With A Conscience*

"Freed is accurate and faithful to Paine at every turn, and I thank him for that; it is rare."

    – KEN BURCHELL, Thomas Paine Historian

"An incredibly well-researched and documented book. Fans of [the film] *What the Bleep Do We Know!?* will get some more ideas from this new book."

    – MARSHA DOYENNE, Essentials Bookstore

"Freed makes his case that in this time of global unrest, we the people must begin a new way of thinking and acting."

    – FOREWORD MAGAZINE

"*Global Sense* weaves together history, ethics, and the battle of the sexes in a friendly, accessible inquiry into our natural rights, liberties, and responsibilities on planet earth.... Freed's theories seem more applicable with the onslaught of each new worldwide crisis.... The author is destined to be touted as one of the great thinkers of our generation."

    – MARK BRODERICK, reviewer, *The Compulsive Reader*

GLOBAL
SENSE

An update of *Common Sense*

YES

GLOBAL SENSE

Awakening Your Personal Power
for Democracy and World Peace

Judah Freed

An update of Thomas Paine's *Common Sense*
to renew hope in these times that try our souls

Foreword by Thom Hartmann
Preface by David Wann
Afterword by Dr. Vandana Shiva

Who's Who, Bibliography and Study Guide

Media Visions Press
Denver, Colorado USA

2006

Global Sense © Copyright 2002-2006 by Kenneth Judah Freed.
Foreword © 2005 by Thom Hartmann. Preface © 2002 by David Wann.
Afterword © 2005 by Dr. Vandana Shiva. Cover & book design © Judah Freed.
Earth photo by Gene Cernan on the 1972 Apollo XVII return flight from the moon.
Published by Media Visions Press, Denver, Colo. USA (MediaVisionsPress.com)
Supports Green Press Initiative: Printed in Canada on 100% Recycled Paper. ♻

eBook edition first published – January 10, 2002.
   (226th anniversary of First edition of *Common Sense*.)
Print softcover trial first edition published – February 14, 2003.
   (227th anniversary of Second edition of *Common Sense*.)
   Revised editions – 2004, 2005, 2006 (was ISBN 0-9728905-1-3)
Print clothcover First edition – Summer 2006.
   (230th Anniversary Year of *Common Sense*.)

TELL US YOUR STORY. If *Global Sense has* helped
you to change yourself and our world, tell us your story!
Your inspiring experiences may be in a follow-up book.
Please send an email: http://mediavisionspress.com/contact/

10 Percent of Author's Profits
Donated to Literacy Projects

Cataloging-in-Publication Data:

Clothcover   ISBN 0-9728905-5-6
Softcover   ISBN 0-9728905-2-1
eBook   ISBN 0-9728905-0-5

Freed, Kenneth Judah, 1950—
   GLOBAL SENSE:
   Awakening Your Personal Power for Democracy and World Peace
   (An update of *Common Sense* by Thomas Paine)
   Foreword by Thom Hartmann. Preface by David Wann.
   Afterword by Dr. Vandana Shiva.

192 pages, 21 chapters.
with Paine bio, who's who, bibliography, study guide, acknowledgements, index.

   1. Contemporary Affairs/Social Issues. 2. Personal Growth/Self Help.
   3. Philosophy/Ethics. 4. Politics/Government. 5. Spirituality/New Age.
   6. Communication. 7. Gender Studies. 8. Literary Essays.

Dedication

*For Thomas Paine, who showed up, paid attention,
told the truth, and let go to Nature's God.
May his old soul smile in peace.*

Common sense is not so common.
    – VOLTAIRE

The price of freedom is eternal vigilance.
— THOMAS JEFFERSON

FOREWORD
What Would Paine Write?
by Thom Hartman

IN MY book *What Would Jefferson Do?* I showed why democracy is not an aberration in human history, but is the oldest, most resilient and most universal form of government, with roots in nature itself.

In the book that you're now holding, *Global Sense,* Judah Freed updates Thomas Paine's classic 1776 essay, *Common Sense,* to show how the universal force of our global interdependence can empower each one of us to help make democracy work—*if* we're willing to do the personal growth needed to manage our freedom responsibly.

Freed asked himself, what would Tom Paine write if he were alive today? The result is a provocative, inspiring essay that promises fresh hope for liberty. *Global Sense* offers practical ideas for transforming the political landscape and reviving Thomas Jefferson's dream of real democracy. We must act before it is too late.

Today, 81 nations can be justly described as fully democratic. Yet in numerous countries around the world, including the United States, democracy has failed or is tottering, and its principles are increasingly under siege from corporate and other authoritarian forces.

The problem is awakening to the root causes behind the rise of an oppressive aristocracy taking over not just the U.S. but also the world. *Global Sense* argues that "male rule" and "authority addiction" are these root causes. You may agree or not, but it's reasonable to say that as enough of us assert our natural personal power for governing our institutions, actual self government becomes more possible.

Paine's and Jefferson's ideal of a genuine democracy representing "we the people" is coming back to life.

Consider the parallels between Paine's day and our own.

The 1773 Boston Tea Party, for example, was a protest against the world's largest transnational corporation, The East India Company, gaining tax-free monopoly power over American trade. Today we see

---

modern multinational corporations, represented by the World Trade Organization and by other bodies, dictating policies to entire nations without a vote by the people effected. A growing fear that democracy is being hijacked by commercial interests has led to "Tea Parties" at world trade meetings in such places as Seattle and Genoa.

As another example, democracy in America came under assault in 1798 when President John Adams pushed through Congress the Alien and Sedition Acts, which turned the U.S. toward authoritarian, single-party rule under the Federalists. Adams closed opposition newspapers and ordered "unpatriotic" opponents arrested. Jefferson repealed the laws when he won the Presidency in 1800, but his victory was slim. Today we can point to attempts by George W. Bush to emulate John Adams by using the USA Patriot Act to subvert the Bill of Rights and turn the U.S. into a one-party state under far-right Republicans.

History shows that when enough people become politically active, they can rescue the soul of any nation from sliding into a corrupt, abusive police state. Now is the time for us again to follow Jefferson's advice: Let us hope for the best as we organize to oppose politicians who believe that campaign lies are defensible, that laws denying our civil rights are acceptable, and that the ends justify the means.

While everything seems to be collapsing around us—ecodamage, genetic engineering, virulent diseases, the end of cheap oil, water shortages, global famine, wars—we can still do something about it. We can create a world that works for us and our children's children. We can look at what is happening to our planet, find the reasons for our culture's blind behavior, and ask how we can fix the problem.

Global Sense can help us awaken our power to do what must be done now. If we retain the vigilance of Thomas Paine as we struggle against the same forces he fought, we shall prevail. – TH

Thom Hartmann is a nationally syndicated talk radio host and the author of more than a dozen books, including *The Last Hours of Ancient Sunlight, Unequal Protection, The Prophet's Way, We the People,* and *What Would Jefferson Do?* For more information, visit: http://thomhartmann.com.

> *For though at times the flame of liberty may*
> *cease to shine, the ember will never expire.*
> — THOMAS PAINE

PREFACE
Safety and Liberty
by David Wann

JUST as Thomas Paine's literary missiles within *Common Sense* intended to incite an overthrow of despotism, so Judah Freed's ideas in *Global Sense* intend to incite a revolution within each one of us— a planetary evolution into real democracy and world peace.

Freed proposes a cultural/political Big Bang. The implosion of our global commonalties, he reasons, is now giving birth worldwide to self empowerment for every global citizen. The essay argues that we can best empower each other by empowering ourselves.

Thinking like Paine, Freed offers common sense reasons why it is pointless to debate between one despot and another, when mindful self rule—purest democracy—is the only way to go.

Freed deftly wrestles with lofty ideas in a clear, eloquent voice, bringing historical lessons and passions down to earth where we can use them. Never dull nor overly academic, the writing is lively, accessible and engaging.

The book will find a wide audience among the change agents worldwide, estimated at 25 to 50 million "cultural creatives" in the U.S. alone. Many in this sector know intuitively what needs to be done. Freed gives the cultural and intellectual underpinnings of words like "freedom" and "democracy," so they can act effectively.

Global Sense is much more than upbeat idealism. The author acknowledges that we're addicted to authority, craving security more than freedom. The breakthrough idea of this important book is that with personal growth, we can have both safety *and* liberty. – DW

David Wann is the co-author of *Affluenza* and *Superbia,* author of *Biologic, Deep Design,* and *The Zen of Gardening in the High and Arid West.*

*In the following pages I offer nothing more than
simple facts, plain arguments, and common sense.*
— THOMAS PAINE

TABLE OF CONTENTS

COMMON SENSE;

ADDRESSED TO THE

INHABITANTS

O F

A M E R I C A,

On the following interefting

S U B J E C T S.

I. Of the Origin and Defign of Government in general, with concife Remarks on the Englifh Conftitution.

II. Of Monarchy and Hereditary Succeffion.

III. Thoughts on the prefent State of American Affairs.

IV. Of the prefent Ability of America, with fome mifcellaneous Reflections.

Man knows no Mafter fave creating HEAVEN,
Or thofe whom choice and common good ordain.

THOMSON.

PHILADELPHIA;

Printed, and Sold, by R. BELL, in Third-Street.

MDCCLXXVI.

[2006]

GLOBAL SENSE

ADDRESSED TO THE

INHABITANTS

OF

OUR WORLD

On the following interesting

S U B J E C T S.

I. Mindful Self Rule and Modern Republics.

II. Male Rule and Authority Addiction.

III. Thoughts on the State of World Affairs.

IV. Our Ability for Democracy and World Peace.

And if it is a despot you would dethrone,
See first that his throne within you is destroyed.
KAHLIL GIBRAN

DENVER
Published by Media Visions Press

MMVI

NOW

> *Had the spirit of prophecy directed the birth*
> *of this production, it could not have brought it forth*
> *at a more seasonable juncture, or a more necessary time.*
> — THOMAS PAINE (2nd edition of *Common Sense*)

INTRODUCTION
Why update Common Sense?

PERHAPS the sentiments contained in the following pages are not yet sufficiently fashionable to procure them general favor. A long habit of not thinking a thing wrong gives it a superficial appearance of being right, and raises at first a formidable outcry in defense of custom. But tumult soon subsides. Time makes more converts than reason.

So Thomas Paine began his introduction to *Common Sense,* which voiced the vision of the Enlightenment movement in the 18th century. Paine's radiant reasoning fits the Global Enlightenment movement of the 21st century. I've updated his essay to help us define a new vision of democracy that puts our highest ideals into practice today.

Back in 1776, a dark time for the friends of freedom, Paine's essay revived hope and inspired action. For all progressives and libertarians today who mourn the loss of freedom, who want to restore democracy by uniting personal growth and politics, this update of *Common Sense* likewise can renew hope and inspire action.

Common Sense persuaded colonial Americans in 1776 to fight for independence. Without Paine's essay, historians agree, the American Revolution would have failed for lack of public support. Kings and other masters, Paine argued, unduly claim for themselves the right to decide our future for us. He believed that an abuse of power calls into question the right of the abuser to hold power. Those suffering abuses have a natural right and a moral duty to reject their abusers.

Similarly, we have a right and a duty examine our personal habits and look into why we worship our rulers. Do we create governments to rule us so we can avoid responsibility for ruling ourselves? In this book we'll expose what I call *authority addiction*. We'll see how our hidden fears drive us to sacrifice liberty for security.

In the pages ahead, we'll see how a global sense of our natural interactivity empowers us to evolve the habits of personal and social responsibility that can sustain democracy and world peace. Indeed, I'll assert, *peace and democracy are personal growth issues.*

I began writing *Global Sense* after the "9/11" attacks in 2001, yet the ideas voiced in the book have been evolving within me for three decades. The writing therefore contains subtle layers of meaning that I hope reveal new delights each time you read the book.

My most difficult task in updating *Common Sense* was expressing Thomas Paine's love for freedom and democracy while shifting his passionate call for national war into a compassionate call for world peace. *I've been transformed by writing this book. My prayer is that you will be transformed by reading it.*

Like Paine, I've chosen to avoid personal comments about today's leaders in this essay, placing principles before personalities. Neither praise nor blame of living persons changes our current situation.

Also, I see no need for pressuring anyone into agreeing with me. Those who now feel hostile to global thinking might one day come to adopt this worldview on their own, unless, as Paine warned,

> too much pain is bestowed on their conversion.

The cause of peaceful democracy is the cause of all humankind. The outcomes of pivotal events in society and the world today affect the interests of all who care about sustaining life on earth.

> Many circumstances have, and will arise, which are not local, but universal.... Laying a country desolate with fire and sword, declaring war against the natural rights of all [hu]mankind, and extirpating the defenders thereof from the face of the earth, is the concern of every [hu]man to whom nature hath given the power of feeling.

Regardless of gender, race, religion, class, or party, a call of alarm for the future of freedom is long overdue. Among those working to rebuild hope for democracy and world peace, gratefully stands,

Judah Freed,
Denver, Colorado
Summer 2006

I. Mindful Self Rule
and Modern Republics

*The discipline of desire is
the background of character.*
— JOHN LOCKE

1. Personal Democracy

FEAR, rage and grief consumed me when two hijacked airplanes slashed into the World Trade Center towers on September 11, 2001. Standing dumbstruck before my television screen at home in Denver, I watched the live news feed from New York at 9:03 AM as United Flight 175 banked gracefully into the south tower and burst into a ball of flame. When the twin towers collapsed that morning, the debris cascading down looked like two inverted mushroom clouds.

As the days wore on, TV news began to echo the drumbeat of war emanating from the White House. Because I've worked for years as a journalist reporting on media and politics, because I've studied and taught the tools of public relations and propaganda, I saw an ominous trend. With Americans feeling terrified, the president was pledging an "endless war on terrorism" while implying the air attack justified a crackdown on U.S. society—for our own safety, of course.

I picked up my phone and called my representatives in Congress. I left messages urging them not to sacrifice our civil liberties on the alter of homeland security. They did not call back.

In the weeks that followed, I began drafting an essay on the future of democracy in America and the world. I wrote that most of us are ripe for plucking by tyrants because we feel afraid and insecure. As I wrote, I confronted my own dark shame and pain, the hidden shadow of self doubt that for years has kept me small and weak.

In late September, I recalled using Thomas Paine's *Common Sense* in 1997 as the framework for an essay at my new website on the need for democratic governance of the Internet. In a flash of insight, I saw that Paine's classic work was a perfect vehicle for talking about how global thinking empowers us for freedom. Inspired by Paine as if he was leaning over my shoulder, whispering in my ear, I started writing this book, voicing my soul while praying to touch your heart.

> **SOME** writers have so confounded society with government, as to leave little or no distinction between them; whereas they are not only different, but [they] have different origins. Society is produced by our wants, and government by our wickedness; the former promotes our happiness positively by uniting our affections, the latter negatively by restraining our vices. The one encourages intercourse, the other creates distinctions. The first is a patron, the last a punisher. Society in every state is a blessing, but government even in its best state is but a necessary evil, in its worst state an intolerable one.

In this way Tom Paine opened *Common Sense*. His ideas still ring true today. By seeing the difference between society and government, we can discover our personal power to shape the future.

The history of society is the story of humanity learning to accept responsibility for liberty. If people governed their own lives sensibly, there would be no need for a high government to control our lowest impulses. If we all lived with compassionate regard for one another, if we loved and respected others as we want to be treated, we'd barely need any government at all. That's not our current reality.

Our reality today is a world filled with hate, violence, exploitation, and suffering. Why? Society reflects the web of mass consciousness woven daily by what we think, say and do. Our daily actions impact ourselves, our families, workplaces, communities, nations, and planet. The harmful habits of our minds and hearts are reflected in society, and society reinforces those harmful habits in us. It's a vicious circle. To break the cycle, we need to transform our consciousness. Happily, such a worldwide change in our thinking is happening now.

In an era of globalization, two specters haunt our world, the spirits of absolute tyranny and genuine democracy. We live in the spectrum between. On one side are corporations and religions ruling us through puppet governments that prey upon our addiction to authority. On the other side is a grassroots movement for peace and democracy through enlightened spiritual awareness of our global oneness. Which way goes society and government depends on which way goes each of us. *Our daily choices decide the fate of life on earth.*

Once we accept our global "interdependence" as a fact of life, as naturally as dawn follows night, we recognize our personal and social responsibility for managing our personalities, our societies and our governments. Acknowledging our innate oneness with life inspires us to live more consciously and cooperatively, so kings or other masters are not needed. Awakening to a global sense of our unity in a diverse community is our best hope for democracy and world peace.

In these times that try our souls, as humanity faces dismal dangers, too many of us make Big Government a social necessity by refusing to practice *mindful self rule* and *personal democracy*. We resent our governments for limiting our freedom, but we glorify forceful power. We praise democracy, but we elect men who would be kings.

Why is there a disconnect between our ideals and our realities?

Robert Putnam in *Bowling Alone* says we've become cut off in our communities from our families, friends, neighbors, and democratic structures. He feels our stock of "social capital" (our connection with one another) has fallen sharply, impoverishing our societies.

Richard Bellah argues in *Habits of the Heart* that modern life has become cut off from healthy feelings of community by "narcissistic individualism." We're so wrapped up in instant gratification that we lack any language to discuss our rights and duties in a republic.

As a solution, I propose reviving the ideas of Thomas Paine and other Enlightenment thinkers. Updated by terms from communication theory and personal growth, we'll gain a neutral vocabulary to discuss how to govern ourselves sensibly in a global society. If we can agree on a fair plan for self government, all humanity might prosper.

SOCIETY has long been ruled by a worldview that makes sense of life by assuming a king must govern us. Now we're evolving a new view of life. Due to the emergence of "global thinking," Paine's 18th century vision of a free society makes sense in our 21st century.

To understand why *Common Sense* made sense at the dawn of the United States, and why it still applies to us today, put yourself in the place of those reading Thomas Paine's essay in 1776.

The colonists' rights as citizens under the English Constitution had been revoked by "mad" King George III, who probably suffered from variegate porphyria.* Parliament only made matters worse with the Stamp Act, Tea Act, and other "intolerable acts." As Thom Hartmann

---

* For more info: http://www.porphyriafoundation.com/about_por/history.htm

chronicled in *Unequal Protection,* Americans hurt by tyranny united behind the protest, "No taxation without representation." The people wanted a fair say in making the laws governing their lives.

Massachusetts rebelled in early 1775, so English ships blockaded Boston Harbor. When British soldiers killed American colonists at nearby Lexington on April 19, this "massacre" confused and terrified Americans in all of the colonies. They likely felt much like modern Americans felt in 2001 after the 9/11 terrorist attacks.

Most colonial Americans expected to reconcile with England and stay under the crown, but a faction wanted to break away. Members of secret "committees of correspondence" wrote letters advocating *independency* for the continent. They were like the writers on Internet blogs and listservs today urging democracy and world peace. Then as now, the friends of liberty struggled to make their case.

Just as Americans learned that King George III had declared all the colonies in rebellion, out of nowhere on January 10, 1776, appeared a pamphlet entitled, *Common Sense.* The public impact was electric. Historians affirm this was the right message at the right time.

Thomas Paine's four-part essay defined the nature of government, rejected monarchy and hereditary succession, told why reconciliation with the king would be irrational, and showed how Americans could win a rebellion against Britain. The essay further urged a declaration of independence and offered a plan for writing a national constitution. As a truly free country founded on democracy, Paine wrote, America would become a beacon of hope for the world.

Common Sense shifted public opinion in favor of the revolution. George Washington said the essay erased his lingering doubts about leading the rebel army. Why was *Common Sense* so powerful?

PAINE distilled into common language the ideas and ideals of the Enlightenment thinkers in the 18th century. Their views flowed from the Age of Reason in the 17th century, which arose from the Protestant Reformation in the 16th century, which sprang from the Renaissance in the 15th century, which revived Greek and Roman philosophy after a millennium of medieval darkness in Europe.

The invention of modern printing had upset the cultural applecart. Popular books on classical thought recalled Plato's wholistic view of life and Aristotle's deconstruction of reality into its tiniest classifiable parts. These books restored the use of reason based on the syllogism: *If A = B, and if B = C, then A = C.* Using logic, "freethinkers" and scientists like Benjamin Franklin applied René Descartes' and Francis Bacon's useful tool for critical thinking—The Scientific Method:

1. Create a working hypothesis or theory from all available facts.
2. Test the hypothesis fairly (tests must be repeatable by others).
3. Impartially and rigorously analyze the test findings.
4. Revise the hypothesis to fit the findings (return to Step 1).

Freethinkers read *The Principia* by Sir Isaac Newton, who saw an apple fall straight to earth (not on his head) and deduced gravitation. Newton supported Copernicus and Galileo, who said our planet goes around the sun. Man on earth was not the center of the universe, as the Church had taught. Reason was gaining power over religion just as the *Magna Carta* had given the law power over the king.

SUCH trends raised a vital question: Can we live without kings?

Thomas Hobbes' 1642 book, *Leviathan,* said that we're all selfish animals at constant war in a world where life is "nasty, brutish, and short." To control our animal impulses, we need absolute kings not subject to any laws, for "might makes right." (Hobbes' views guided Big Brother in George Orwell's novel, *Nineteen Eight-Four.* Hobbes likely would praise today's "homeland security" laws.)

Baruch Spinoza shared Hobbes' cynicism, yet his 1677 *Ethics* saw benefits from more individuality and civil liberties. Spinoza imagined society providing so much gratification that state oppression was not needed to keep us in line. (His views guided Aldous Huxley's novel, *Brave New World,* where people are soothed by *soma.* Spinoza likely would praise the media banality mollifying the masses today.)

For the record, Spinoza later influenced Friedrich Nietzsche, heir to amoral Machiavelli. Nietzsche promoted individual autonomy and a "superman" ruled only by ambition and expedience (a moral stance adopted by Nazism), where the only sin is getting caught. We see this utilitarian morality today in those seeking power at any cost.

Countering justifications for tyranny in the Age of Reason were voices of hope for our human potential in the Enlightenment.

John Locke's 1690 *Two Treatises on Civil Government* said people and the state are ruled by *natural law.* In nature, each of us is free and equal, although different. We're each our own moral judge. Moral self discipline must guide the "pursuit of happiness," which sensibly leads to cooperation, not competition. Our selfish urges naturally give way to a regard for the common good. (In modern management lingo, just as Hobbes favored "Theory X," Locke favored "Theory Y.")

Government is powerless without the consent of the people, Locke said. To protect us from a state abusing its power, he advocated the principle of *checks and balances* in government constitutions.

If any state represses or denies the citizens' natural rights, Locke asserted, a revolution in such cases is not only our civil right under natural law, but it may be our moral duty.

Locke influenced Jean Jacques Rousseau, who in 1762 published *The Social Contract*. "Nature never deceives us," he wrote; "it is we who deceive ourselves." Yet nature lacks morality or law in itself, so good people exist only if society makes them good through a social contract. Prone to competition, we may *agree* to cooperate.

Rousseau urged a "social compact" for democracy, warning that the majority is *not* always right. What is right? Religious and political morals often conflict, and religious leaders tend to abuse their power. So, he called for the *separation of church and state.*

Rousseau favored moral self mastery. "Never exceed your rights," he wrote, "and they will soon become unlimited."

If a state acts in an immoral way, Rousseau said, that government violates its social contract and ceases to be legitimate, losing the right to wield authority over us. "Force does not constitute right; obedience is due only to legitimate powers." Fully convinced that might does *not* make right, Rousseau agreed with Locke that if the state loses its legitimacy, a revolution becomes a public necessity.

Inspired by Locke, Rousseau and other Enlightenment thinkers, Paine said in *Common Sense* that British rule in America had become illegitimate. He called for a violent regime change. His essay struck a resonant chord. The people responded with passion.

MANY of us today think our leaders in the U.S. and in other lands likewise have broken the social contract by waging corrupt wars, by revoking our civil liberties, by abetting environmental destruction in a heedless pursuit of profits. We contend that our governments are no longer morally legitimate. Yet we call for a *peaceful* regime change, for we know that the real revolution starts within ourselves.

Criticism of the government is not enough to cause social change. Without a realistic vision of a better world to inspire us with hope, we will not do the inner growth work that yields cultural shifts. This book is my contribution towards that empowering global vision. I advocate "mindful self rule" and "personal democracy." What do I mean?

Mindful self rule is the fine art of making ethical or moral choices about how we want to live. For example, when I've chosen over the years to recover from addictions to tobacco and debting, that's a form of mindful self rule. When I've chosen to sit beside a river to feel inner peace and commune with the God of my understanding, that's a form of mindful self rule. When I've chosen in the privacy of my heart to honor my family, friends and neighbors as equal souls with free will, that's definitely an act of mindful self rule.*

Personal democracy is the art of expressing mindful self rule in the world. If you seek a job in accord with your social or ecological values, that's personal democracy. If you boycott products made with slave labor, that's personal democracy. If you volunteer in a school or literacy center, that's personal democracy. If you protest abuses of our human rights, that's personal democracy. If you vote your conscience on election day, that's definitely an act of personal democracy.

Inner self rule and outer personal democracy interact. In Taoism, the feminine *yin* energy stimulates masculine *yang* energy as *yang* stimulates *yin*, forming a dynamic loop. In the very same way, self rule stimulates personal democracy as personal democracy stimulates self rule.

What if our inner choices and outer actions are in conflict? Takeo Doi describes our struggles in *The Anatomy of Self.* Japanese culture, for example, marks a difference between outer face (*omote*) and inner truth (*ura*). Social standards and mores (*tatemae*) may disagree with our inner knowledge of what is natural and right (*honne*). Conflicts between the self and the society twist us into knots. A need to resolve the tension, I know from experience, makes us gullible to the appeals of shoguns, messiahs and other masters promising us the soft comfort of mindless obedience—the opposite of mindful self rule.

Practicing mindful self rule and personal democracy hinges upon understanding the nature and power of *communication*. We'll see in Chapter 15 how we use communication to make sense of our lives

---

* I have deliberately decided in this book *not* to hyphenate "self-rule" and related compound terms, so we'll be more alert to the autonomy of the individual self.

and our world. We'll learn how splitting our perceptions lets us filter out awareness of unpleasant truths about ourselves, such as how our self hate gets twisted into hatred toward others.

What matters here is knowing that we each form our personalities and societies through all the ways we interact daily. *Changing how we communicate changes the world where we communicate.* So, treating others with more love actually creates a more loving world.

On this planet where we each live and breathe and have our being, we each are a "co-creator." What we do to others, we do to ourselves. We may admire the Golden Rule, but do we live accordingly?

Global interactivity means that each of us is globally powerful, perhaps infinitely powerful. *Saying we are powerless is our excuse to avoid responsibility for using our global power wisely.*

If love is the glue that holds life together, expanding our capacity for love expands global unity. Seeking inner peace helps create world peace. Liberating ourselves liberates the world. This is why Benjamin Franklin said, "Who is powerful? He that governs his passions."

IN THIS opening chapter, I've laid a philosophical foundation for the update of *Common Sense* that follows. This was needed because schools rarely explain abstract ideals like "freedom" or "democracy." We rarely hear that *we can change the world by changing ourselves.* So, what's the plan from here?

In Part I, where Paine looked at the nature of civil government, we'll apply his ideas to self rule and personal democracy.

In Part II, where Paine refuted monarchy and hereditary succession, we'll challenge "male rule" and "authority addiction."

In Part III, where Paine argued against serving a king, we'll argue against enabling authority addiction in the world or in ourselves.

In Part IV, where Paine showed how to win national independence, we'll see how to use our global interdependence to win world peace.

In other words, the first half of this book identifies our common problems, and the second half suggests practical solutions. If you stay with me on this journey, you will feel more empowered.

Our goal is self liberation. A free society follows.

Government is not reason; it is not eloquent; it is force.
Like fire, it is a dangerous servant and a fearful master.
– GEORGE WASHINGTON

2. Origin and Rise of Government

WE SUFFER in many lands on earth from the actions of our own governments. Our troubles look worse in our eyes when we see how we supplied the means of our suffering by consenting to be ruled by these bad governments. As Thomas Paine wrote,

Government, like dress, is the badge of lost innocence. The palaces of kings are built on the ruins of the bowers of paradise. For were the impulses of conscience clear, uniform, and irresistibly obeyed, we would need no other lawgiver.

Everyone heeding the universal *still small voice* of God within us would render all governments obsolete. Tyranny, therefore, would be pointless. Given our fears of anarchy, however, we create government by the same prudent reasoning that advises us, when faced by two evils, to choose the least evil.

In my early twenties, for example, I was so profoundly confused and emotionally needy that I joined an authoritarian religious cult for almost three years. Looking back now, more than 30 years later, I see how my decision to leave that cult launched me onto a spiritual path toward journalism and world service as a liberty advocate. My choice to serve a master, rather than practice self mastery, points to why we need to understand the principles behind politics.

One of Paine's earliest tasks in *Common Sense* was explaining the nature of government. As a progressive libertarian, he believed that protecting us from force and fraud is the first purpose of government, but leaders must not use force or fraud to stay in power. Because we choose external government over internal self rule, we surrender part of our property and privacy, such as taxes and airport searches, so the state has the means to protect our possessions and our lives.

Paine said the best form of government is the one most likely to secure our freedom at the least expense.

TO EXPLAIN the origin of government, Paine offered a *parable*:

> Let us suppose a small number of persons settled in some
> sequestered part of the earth.... They will then represent the
> first peopling of any country, or of the world. In this state of
> natural liberty, society will be their first thought.

Human beings are social animals innately unfit for eternal solitude.
Since thousands of urges excite each person, and since people cannot
satisfy all desires by themselves, the colonists soon feel bound to seek
help and relief from one another. Self sufficiency is valued, yet talents
are most easily noticed through service to neighbors. Adversity forges
common bonds as feelings of unity arise among the settlers.

Driven by social necessity, the emigrants form a loose community.
Rights and duties are spread fairly among everyone as relative equals.
Whatever culture may emerge in that remote place, the blessings from
mutual integrity make the limits of law and government unnecessary.
The people don't need a government, for they practice *self rule*. Their
utopian anarchy lasts only as long as they behave themselves.

Impermanence might be the one permanent truth in our universe.
The settlers' initial struggles united them in common cause, yet in that
first generation or another, human frailties and vices surface, such as
robbery, rape or murder. Seeing others sin, the resolve for self control
evaporates. As a distrust spreads, the settlers discover the necessity of

> establishing some form of government to supply the defect
> of moral virtue.

The settlers decide they need a government to rule them because
they cannot or will not rule themselves without a government.

> Some convenient tree will afford them a State House.
> Under its branches the whole colony may assemble to
> deliberate on public matters.... In this first parliament every
> [hu]man, by natural right will have a seat.

Thus, the people form a "direct" or *genuine democracy*.

Most likely, the first laws will carry the muted titles of Guidelines.
Regulations will follow. The early laws may be enforced by a penalty
no more severe than social disdain—the old cold shoulder.

As the population grows, community concerns increase. But some members now live too far away to attend all meetings at the Council Tree. Personal inconvenience creates a communication barrier—the first block to all of the people participating in their democracy.

When meetings grow too unwieldy, people discover the necessity of agreeing to leave the job of lawmaking to a few wise heads, chosen by the community. Power shifts from the people to their leaders.

The new assembly of delegates has the same concerns and interests as the people electing them. These representatives vote the same way as the whole body would act if they all were present. Under this new social contract, the people form a *representative democracy*. To use the correct term, they form a simple *republic*.

With the population growing, new districts need to be represented. The legislature adds seats. Each district elects its representatives, who vote as the majority in the district would vote if they all were present. In this way, any republic may prosper honorably in the land.

To stop the representatives from forming any interest groups apart from the common electorate, Paine wrote,

> prudence will point out the propriety of having elections often; those elected may by that means return and mix again with the general body of electors every few months; their fidelity to the [voting] public will be secured by the prudent reflection of not making a rod for themselves.

Paine was alluding to corporal punishment. He meant that corrupt officials give their foes a reason to beat them at the polls.

Lively, open speech between the electors and elected, Paine knew, helps representatives stay connected with all parts of the community being represented. The electors and elected, therefore,

> mutually and naturally support each other, and on this (not on the unmeaning name of [a] king) depends the strength of government, and the happiness of the governed.

Our imagined state is now two steps removed from self rule. The people have grown reliant on government for choices they once made themselves, like when to plant a field and how to price the grain. Life in a republic diverts people from recalling life in a direct democracy. Soon their memories of living without any government vanish.

In time, even the basic tasks of a proxy democracy in the republic seem alien and futile. If people believe money buys the ballot box, that their votes do not count, they stop voting. People swallow bland public policy pabulum because they feel powerless. They lose hope. As apathy spreads, power shifts even further to the leaders.

Without deep feelings of community to sustain the social contract, people forget about self control or self realization. They indulge their lowest appetites. The people turn numb to suffering in themselves and others. They forget about compassion and mercy.

As the government loses accountability, access to leaders is tightly controlled. Those few people who bother to complain or protest are punished. When free speech dies, the social contract between voters and leaders fails. The bonds of community finally snap.

A communication breakdown between government and the people breeds revolt. Chaos ensues as communication failures multiply. With a promise to restore law and order, a charismatic leader arises to be a king. The people give up their civil liberties for the sake of security. Soon they forget the meaning of "freedom." They are willing slaves who cannot be free because they do not know they have a choice.

PAINE'S parable shows how any "nation state" can migrate from individual *self rule* to a direct *democracy* to a representative *republic* and then slide into *tyranny*. The foothold of freedom stands forever on a slippery slope. As his words prove, Thomas Paine understood and championed the value of personal democracy.

> Here then is the origin and rise of government, namely, a mode rendered necessary by the inability of [individual] moral virtue to govern the world; here too is the design and end of government, *viz,** freedom and security.
>
> And however our eyes may be dazzled with snow, or our ears deceived by sound; however prejudice may warp our wills, or interest darken our understanding, the simple voice of nature and of reason will say, it is right.

---

* From the Latin *videlicit*, one may see. In the 18th century, *viz* meant "namely."

The fundamental principle of a free government
is the equal representation of a free people

— Mercy Otis Warren

3. Constitutional Republics

INDIVIDUALS need a system of moral rules to govern their lives responsibly. For governments, such rules are called constitutions.

> I draw my idea of the form of government from a principle in nature, which no art can overturn, *viz,* that the more simple any thing is, the less liable it is to be disordered, and the easier repaired when disordered.

In this way Thomas Paine launched his discussion of the English constitutional monarchy in 1776. I'll paraphrase him in this chapter to speak about the constitutional republic in the United States today. We'll apply Paine's insights to other nations in the next chapter. The principles of national government equally apply to self government, and we'll tie these together throughout the book.

The U.S. Constitution—while inspired by Athenian democracy, the Roman republic and the Iroquois confederacy—primarily was modeled after the English Constitution. Both are noble documents, given the dark and slavish times when they arose. In a world ruled by absolute kings, the British and American constitutional democracies appeared on earth like a glorious divine rescue from despotism.

> But that it [the Constitution] is imperfect, subject to convulsions, and incapable of producing what it seems to promise, is easily demonstrated.

The British and American social contracts are the flawed products of political compromise deals. As a result, each system of government is so exceedingly complex that the people

> may suffer [abuses] for years together without being able to discover in which part the fault lies; some will say in one [part] and some in another, and every political physician will advise a different medicine.

If the prescription is public safety, Paine wrote, the only means for a government to guarantee total security is to turn totalitarian.

> Absolute governments (though the disgrace of human nature) have this advantage with them, that they are simple; if the people suffer, they know the head from which their suffering springs, know likewise the remedy, and are not bewildered by a variety of causes and cures.

A solution is self evident. First, remove the master from authority. Since absolutist leaders rely on cult psychology to retain power, the second step is helping the True Believers give up groupthink. In time, those programmed to obey learn to trust their own wisdom.

Liberty is not the tradition in every land. Where representative or republican democracy has become a habitual way of life, the ongoing personal growth needed for genuine democracy is difficult. It's hard to release a long-standing, comfortable prejudice for wanting leaders to control our lives. Responsible self rule frightens most of us.

LET US examine the parts of the American Constitution, as Paine did for the English Constitution. We immediately find traces of two medieval tyrannies, adapted to modern republican tastes.

First, the remains of monarchical tyranny reside in the office of the president and the executive branch, modeled on Britain's king and his court, which was ruled by decree.

Second, traces of aristocratic tyranny endure in the U.S. Senate, modeled on Britain's House of Lords, the nobility.

Serving the common people is the U.S. House of Representatives, modeled on Britain's House of Commons. The true republican spirit still dwells in these American and British legislatures. On their virtue rest our best hope for preserving democracy.

The Senate and House combined form the United States Congress, mirroring Britain's combined Parliament. Each assembly in America and Britain is a majestic body. Sadly, those elected to these bodies too often contribute too little to our actual freedom and prosperity.

Now focus on the U.S. system. A president can serve two four-year terms. Senators can serve unlimited six-year terms. Representatives can serve unlimited two-year terms. Because private wealth funds their campaigns, they are not beholding to the common voters. They feel little affinity for those persuaded to elect them. They're supposed to maintain frequent contact with voters at home to keep their seats. Instead, they devote far more time to fundraising than to lawmaking. Their interests lie apart from those they represent.

PRESIDENTIAL power is checked by the Congress. The Senate ratifies cabinet and court appointments while the House approves a president's budget. The Constitution gives the president a countering power to check Congress with a veto of their legislation. A so-called " balance of powers" exists because, as Paine wrote,

> A [chronic] thirst for absolute power is the natural disease of monarchy.

Yet in fairness, we must concede that this constitutional system of *checks and balances* is based on two contradictory presumptions. The veto provision assumes that the president is wiser than all of those in Congress, but the right to approve appointments and budgets assumes that Congress is wiser than the president. How can each be wiser than the other? Paine declared that this same illogical disparity between the British crown and Parliament was a "mere absurdity!"

And there's a ludicrous aspect to the job of the presidency itself. Presidents are encircled by layers of protective buffers, much like in Jonathan Swift's *Gulliver's Travels,* where tiny Lilliputian "flappers" must move the king's lips and ears before he can communicate. In the same way, the president is cut off from hearing about alternate policy options, yet the president has the power to act in cases that require the most informed judgment possible. Notice the contradiction.

Security for a president isolates the high leader from the world, but the business of being president requires that leader to know the world intimately. Opposing and undermining one another, these conflicting demands for *security* and *access* must make the routine character of the presidency feel surreal at times. The confusion must inevitably confound sound decision-making in the White House.

Also, the private interests backing the election of a president often filter out options of higher merit that do not serve their cause or their ideology. The president winds up in a self-contained echo chamber. As a consequence, short-sighted policies prevail. A president's work product can be ineffective at best or destructive at worst.

THE third important U.S. constitutional "power center" is the Supreme Court and federal judges, which can check the president and Congress if either abuses their authority.

Supreme Court justices and federal judges are appointed for life. They are nominated by presidents and approved by the Senate. The House has *no* vote in court appointments. Why not? Was the judiciary ever intended to feel any allegiance to the common people?

The Supreme Court, like high courts in most nations, reflects the same legacy from feudalism as the president and the Senate. The term "court" itself derives from monarchy. Willful kings in court chambers once settled all disputes. (Remember King Solomon?) We can thank angry English barons in 1215 for the *Magna Carta*. Their insistence on curbing an abusive monarch gave to us the modern moral and political principle of a leader ruled by the law.

Politics create the laws before they reach the courts, which apply the laws. In a republic or democracy, judges must stay within the law, uphold trial by jury, and ignore political bias. Judicial independence is the best guarantor of *equal justice under the law*.

Does the U.S. Supreme Court embody fairness? In the close 2000 presidential election, the Democratic candidate won the popular vote. Then Fox News preemptively reported a Republican win in crucial Florida. The High Court intervened to stop a disputed Florida recount, effectively selecting a president instead of letting voters elect one.

If the Supreme Court had not acted, an Electoral College deadlock was possible. In that event, the Constitution provides for the House of Representatives to decide the election. Because the Republican Party controlled the House in 2000, the GOP still would have won, but the House was denied its due vote under the Constitution. Was the High Court's action unconstitutional? Like the discounted and uncounted voters in Florida, were all Americans disenfranchised?

Is the U.S. Supreme Court a trustworthy body? Do the president's appointees erode our trust? Will today's Supreme Court ever reverse such unconstitutional measures as those in the Patriot Act?

LIKE Paine wrote about the English Constitution, it's a fallacy to say the U.S. Constitution is a balanced union of three separate powers —executive, legislative, judicial—reciprocally checking one another.

The phrase "separation of powers" rarely has real meaning beyond symbolic rhetoric. Cases may be cited where one government branch stopped abuses by another branch, but do not be fooled.

U.S. President Dwight D. Eisenhower in the 1950s, for instance, ordered all of his administration officials to stop testifying before the "unAmerican activities" committee of Sen. Joe McCarthy, the surly pursuer of communists in America; his tactics mirrored his foes in Moscow. When "Ike" cut off political support, McCarthy was primed for prime-time TV demolition by Edward R. Morrow and a free press. The "witch hunts" ended. The "blacklists" ended.

But Eisenhower acted only after McCarthy publicly humiliated a presidential war buddy. McCarthyism was halted only by personality politics, *not* by the Constitution. This was far better than no restraints at all on power and ambition. However, please observe the failure by "the rule of law" in curbing that nascent dictatorship in America.

More recently, Republicans in Congress told K Street lobbyists in Washington, DC, to hire only Republican staffers and contribute only to Republican campaigns, or else they'd be denied access to majority GOP legislators. This "pay to play" scheme was uncovered in 2004, and a top lobbyist went to jail for corruption, but know that nothing in the Constitution has ever halted such abuses of power.

MANY people hail the press or "fourth estate" as the final check on governmental abuses. Given media owners' private interests, can the corporate media be counted as an objective guardian of the public interest? Where is the line between "fair and balanced" reporting or biased propaganda? And do we get the whole story?

When 3,000 people died in Al Qaeda's air attacks against the U.S. on Sept. 11, 2001, press coverage lasted for months. When U.S.-led troops invaded Afghanistan in January 2002, the first U.S. death saw more press coverage than the 3,000 Afghanis killed. The American press spotlighted the death of the 2,000th U.S. soldier in Iraq since the 2003 invasion, but the press has barely reported estimates of 200,000 Iraqi deaths since the invasion. In fact, the U.S. Government does not keep track of Iraqi deaths. *Are not all lives equal?*

Given the consolidation of media ownership into fewer and fewer hands, the diversity of editorial viewpoints is dwindling. Once a free press voiced different perspectives from across the political spectrum.

Now newspapers, magazines, radio, and TV seem to cover the same stories the same way. Why? The so-called "liberal" media are largely owned by conservatives allied with friends in government.

We can learn from a joke I made up decades ago. How many top government officials and media moguls does it take to screw in a light bulb? None. They want to keep the people in the dark.

Nazi propagandist Joseph Goebbels said, "It is the absolute right of the state to supervise the formation of public opinion." His tactic was to repeat a simplistic Big Lie loud enough and often enough until the people believed it. For instance, Hitler's media said Poland posed a threat, so a "preemptive" invasion was justified. After weak Poland was easily occupied in 1939, Hitler said the invasion was necessary anyway. Does this sound like U.S. statements about the "preemptive" invasion of Iraq? Is the similarity a coincidence?

Why don't journalists with integrity protest being used as tools of propaganda? Because speaking truth to power is risky. Reporters soon learn which stories their editors will not publish. Objecting to censorship, I've learned first-hand, can cost reporters their jobs. This causes reporters to practice "self censorship" to keep earning a living, which is the most insidious form of press repression.

Without the press as our watchdog to report government misdeeds, state abuses of constitutional power too rarely are stopped by public outcry. That's a shame. As Paddy Chayefsky advised, we need to tell government officials and media network executives that we're as mad as hell, and we're not going to take it anymore!

WE'VE exposed the hoax that a balance of powers exists between the legislative, executive and judicial branches of government. We've punctured the myth that the mainstream press is our civic guardian. Now take these insights and apply them to mindful self rule.

We might wish to believe that a balance of powers exists between the mental, emotional, physical, and spiritual aspects of ourselves, but in most of us, that's not the case. For years I suffered from a pretense that my life was in balance, but that was a lie. I pretended to be well and whole, but inside myself raged a bitter war.

Whenever a separation is made between liberty
and justice, neither, in my opinion, is safe.
— EDMUND BURKE

4. A House Divided Against Itself

SINCE young adulthood, I've struggled inside between my higher calling for world service and my deep fears about being good enough to make any difference. I've voiced my ideals in conversations and in my journal, but in real life, I've squandered my talents in the squalor of self doubt. Fear of failure and fear of success both restrained me. I've let my childhood wounds rule my life like a tyrant. My shadow self has been one thing and my higher self another.

Could we similarly explain the undemocratic aspects of the U.S. Constitution by saying the government is one thing and the people another? If the U.S. Presidency, Senate and Supreme Court are bodies in behalf of privilege, and if the House of Representatives alone is a body in behalf of the common people, then just as Thomas Paine said about the British constitutional system, the U.S. system has

all the distinctions of an house divided against itself.

Witty words ignoring this conflict may be pleasantly arranged, wrote Paine, but since the conflict does exist, the most clever words,

though they may amuse the ear, cannot inform the mind, for this explanation includes a previous question, *viz*, how came the king [or government] by a power which the people are afraid to trust, and [are] always obliged to check?

Such a power could not be the gift of a wise people, neither can any power, which needs checking, be from God; yet the provision [for political checks and balances], which the constitution makes, supposes such a power to exist.

But the provision [to stop abuse of power] is unequal to the task; the means either cannot or will not accomplish the end, and the whole affair is a *felo de se*.*

---

* Latin for "felon from self," a criminal act causing the death of the felon, like a robber shooting a gun at the pursuing police, who shoot back with deadly force.

The constitutional provisions for a balance of powers are innately imbalanced in most nations. Fated to self destruct like machine gears that do not mesh quite right, government bodies are prevented in most countries from keeping abuse of power in check. We give lip service to civility and fairness, but instead we live in conflict. The same goes for our inner selves. We live in constant conflict. Why?

We cling to a primitive model of authority—compulsive reliance on competitive *alpha male rule.* Can you name a single government on earth today allowing us to live without a defacto king? Even if the leader is a woman, she's usually exhibiting alpha male traits.

Imagine literate and enlightened people able and willing to govern themselves responsibly in a free and open society. As I write this, the United States, Canada, Great Britain and the European Union, Japan, Australia, New Zealand, Israel, India, South Africa, or even Uruguay, seem closest to the ideals of liberty and equal justice for all under the law. But all of these nations fall short. *The most ethical representative republics can only begin to hint at the creative vitality and prosperity possible through genuine democracy.*

UNDER the same natural law that governs our physical universe, every government obeys the laws of mechanics. This principle brings us to Thomas Paine's famous machine metaphor:

> For as the greater weight will always carry up the less [on a pulley], and as all the wheels of a machine are put in motion by one, it only remains to know which power in the constitution has the most weight, for that will govern.
>
> [Other machine parts may retard the weight's motion,] yet so long as they cannot stop it, their endeavors will be ineffectual; the first moving power will at last have its way, and what it wants in speed is supplied by time.
>
> That the crown is this overbearing part in the English constitution needs not be mentioned, and that it derives its whole consequence merely from being the giver of palaces and pensions is self evident; wherefore, though we have been wise enough to shut and lock a door against absolute monarchy, we at the same time have been foolish enough to put the crown in possession of the key.

May the same be said about modern Americans' faith in the U.S. Constitution? The prejudice of U.S. citizens for a government by the president, legislature and courts springs as much from national pride as from reason. Is this not true for other national charters?

Individuals have been safer and more free in America and western Europe than in almost any other land, one may argue. This surely was true until the war on terrorism. Now the whims of the U.S. President become the law of the land easily as the decrees of King George III back in 1776. Instead of the law streaming from a monarch's mouth, now it is handed down in the form of an Executive Order. Either way, people worldwide are effected, and they do not get any vote.

A president also may decree U.S. laws indirectly by calling for an Act of Congress. Granted, a president's bill rarely exits Congress as it entered, and Congress can override a presidential veto with effort. Yet cooperation by Congress often depends less on the common good than a president's personality and clout. Besides, any law a president does sign may be reversed or changed by a Signing Statement.

Why? We pray to be ruled by some shining hero anointed as our savior king (even when a woman wears the crown). Our craving for acceptance and approval by a monarch or master can easily betray us into bondage. Here Paine recalls King Charles I, saying his sorry fate

hath only made kings more subtle, not more just.

Charles I was well-known to any 18th century American with even minimal cultural literacy. Born into Stuart arrogance, Charles seldom walked a straight path if he could find a crooked one, say historians. His saga climaxed in the 1640s. After long disregard for the *Magna Carta* – like secret star chamber courts—public resentment climaxed in the Puritan Revolution. When Charles led his armed troops into the rebellious Parliament, he sparked the English Civil War.

When finally defeated, Charles I was beheaded in 1649. Order was imposed by Puritan Oliver Cromwell, the most bloody, repressive dictator that Britain and Ireland have ever suffered. Out of the frying pan into the inferno. Such terror awaits those in any country split by political extremes when one dictatorship replaces another.

Pushing people into relentless retaliation is never smart. Extremist Islamic terrorist cults are learning this lesson to their grief as America pursues their destruction. American leaders likewise are learning the futility of trying to end the insurgency in Iraq with more troops and more repression. Still learning this lesson are the Arab leaders seeking the destruction of Israel and the Israeli leaders blocking Palestinian statehood. We can say the same about the conflicts between the races. The dreadful cycle of retaliation only fuels our feuds, passing hatred and violence from generation to generation.

Charles' fate also applies to those consolidating corporate wealth and power into a few hands. If the trend continues, expect revolts by suppressed people who've tasted the good life then lost it. And expect rebellion by those in poverty who've never tasted the good life while seeing media images of the elites living lavishly at their expense. The widening gap between rich and poor, the haves and have-nots, clearly destabilizes society, inflicting wounds and breeding resentments that only the justice of widespread affluence can cure.

By persisting in the habits of authoritarian alpha male rule (white male rule), by giving power to the rich and leaving most of us with few rights, if any, we are planting the proverbial dragon's teeth that will sprout soldiers of retribution for generations to come.

Regardless of the offenses against us, let us avoid vengeful urges. Violence on any side hurts all sides. The fate of Charles I gives pause to the ambitious but good-hearted. His story also can turn the cynical sinister, as Paine warned, which causes our authoritarian leaders to be more cunning, not more just (as we'll see in the next chapter).

WE FACE shared threats to freedom and peace in our world, but as Henry David Thoreau wrote, we "lead lives of quiet desperation." We go along to get along while hating ourselves for living a lie. We're so strained and stained by inner conflict that living a life of honor and goodness looks impossible. If we lose hope, we lose power.

For too many years, I've been part of what Amy Goodman calls the "silenced majority." Fearing rejection and ridicule, I've kept my ideas about freedom to myself. Whenever I've felt ready to speak up, my insecurity and shame have arisen to stop me in my tracks.

Given the dangers facing our world today, however, I no longer can stay silent and stay true to my soul. I can't keep living in conflict within like a house divided against itself. Can you?

Those who would give up essential liberty
to purchase a little temporary safety
deserve neither liberty nor safety
— BENJAMIN FRANKLIN

5. Clear and Present Dangers

AT THIS point in *Common Sense* where Thomas Paine discussed the clear and present dangers facing American colonists, let us discuss the real dangers now facing America and our whole world.

Any thinking person may concede three self-evident facts:

1. The United States and European Union have foes around the world who will spit hate at the West with their dying breaths.

2. Since the Al Qaeda attacks on Sept. 11, 2001, we've witnessed a loss of our civil liberties in the name of fighting terrorism.

3. The global war on terrorism has spawned many more terrorists, and each assault on these terrorists only swells their ranks.

Thus, we have given up our natural rights and liberties to purchase a little temporary safety, and our supposed safety is an illusion. Paine wrote that protecting the people is the primary duty of government, but can government protection go too far?

AFTER the 9/11 Al Qaeda attacks on the World Trade Center in New York and the Pentagon in Washington, DC, President George W. Bush declared an "endless war on terrorism." Congress hastily passed a barely debated resolution against terrorism. (The bill was eerily akin to the barely debated 1964 Gulf of Tonkin Resolution that unofficially declared war on Southeast Asia, starting in Vietnam.)

President George W. Bush began using the linguistically subtle term "Homeland Security" and Congress picked up the jargon. Under that slogan, Bush set in motion a plan from The Project for the New American Century (PNAC), created by close allies of past presidents Richard M. Nixon and George H.W. Bush, his father. Aiming to finish the 1991 Gulf War against Iraq and to secure U.S. world supremacy, PNAC's "neoconservative" leaders masterminded the 2000 and 2004 elections of son George W. They serve as his vice president, Secretary of Defense and in other top jobs. Their actions raise questions:

• Did W. Bush ignore early spy service warnings about Al Qaeda planning an air attack to justify the war planned by PNAC?

• After 9/11 (as the 2002 Downing Street memos document), did Bush illegally fabricate evidence about Al Qaeda having ties to Iraq and then lie about Iraq having weapons of mass destruction (WMDs)? Is this why he invaded Iraq before United Nations weapons inspectors had enough time to prove Iraq no longer had such weapons?

• Did Bush approve illegally leaking the identity of the CIA wife of a diplomat who exposed Bush lies about Iraq gaining WMDs?

• Did Bush illegally approve the use of chemical weapons in Iraq?

• Did Bush illegally approve detaining and torturing war prisoners?

• Did Bush criminally violate U.S. law by authorizing the National Security Agency to wiretap American citizens without any warrant?

• Has Bush violated constitutional separations of church and state to promote his brand of Christianity? Has he illegally ordered the IRS and FBI to investigate congregations led by dissenting clergy?

• Has Bush violated the Constitution with his Signing Statements that nullify or distort the Congressional legislation he signs?

• Did Bush corruptly compel tax cuts for the wealthiest Americans (despite the largest budget deficits and national debt in U.S. history) while urging Congress to cut the safety net for the poor?

• Did Bush effectively steal the 2004 election by voter suppression and voting machine tampering in Ohio, Florida and elsewhere?

• Should George W. Bush (and his cronies) be impeached?

SIX weeks after 9/11, the USA PATRIOT Act, a 342-page bill, was passed with *no debate* by the Congress and signed by the president. The cunning acronym means, "Uniting and Strengthening America by Providing Appropriate Tools Required to Intercept and Obstruct Terrorism." May God help those doubting the act's patriotism.

Typical of the law is the so-called "sneak and peek" provision that applies to any person identified as a suspect under the 1978 Foreign Intelligence Surveillance Act (FISA). With a secret warrant from the secret FISA court, agents can enter any location when no one is there to "search for and seize any property or material that constitutes evidence of a criminal offense in violation of the laws of the United States." The FISA suspect may never discover that a "legal" seizure by federal agents was not an illegal burglary by sneaky thieves.

Further, federal judges retain authority to issue secret subpoenas for library, bookstore, Internet, and telephone records of suspects.* Federal agents also may install surveillance "devices or processes" anywhere within the U.S. to record every conversation, phone call, fax, email, and website visit of FISA suspects. Lamentably, under the 2006 Congressional extension of the Patriot Act, key sections of the "temporary" law have now become permanent.

This is only the beginning of intrusive government surveillance. The National Intelligence Reform Act of 2004 (Patriot Act II) erased more civil liberties. The proposed "Total Information Awareness" law would let the government monitor *all* electronic communications by *every* U.S. resident. Good-bye privacy! George Washington wrote, "It will be found an unjust and unwise jealousy to deprive a man of his natural liberty upon the supposition he may abuse it."

DOES labeling any group as evil "bad guys" give the government a right to treat them unfairly or to deny their natural rights?

Civil libertarians say the Patriot Acts violate Constitutional rights of free speech, peaceful assembly, due process, trial by jury, and equal protection. They say the acts void bans against unreasonable searches and seizures as well as cruel and unusual punishments.

Concerns about our rights also apply to the "security certificates" in Canada and the "control orders" in Britain. In fact, terrorism is now being cited as the excuse for revoking civil liberties worldwide, like in Russia, Burma, Nepal, the Sudan, and elsewhere.

When our leaders promise to "hunt down the terrorists and kill them before they kill us," are we willing to forfeit the presumption of innocence and negate the right to a fair trial in open court?

When people are secretly detained and tortured, are we willing to forego warrants based upon probable cause? Are we willing to forego *habeas corpus,* to let governments imprison people for years without charges, without bail, without an attorney, and without any real trial? Alexander Hamilton said, "Arbitrary imprisonments have been, in all ages, the favorite and most formidable instruments of tyranny."

We are told that the new security laws are temporary, but nowhere in the new laws of the U.S. and other nations is there any *guarantee* that our civil rights one day will be fully restored. Why not? Is this

---

* A federal court in 2004 struck down the Internet and phone records portion of the Patriot Act, but the provision remains in force pending government appeals.

because any secret police powers, once obtained, however obtained, are never willingly surrendered by the police? More critically, did we *want* the restructuring of our governments onto a fear-based "endless war" footing? Why not ask us first? Why have citizens in the U.S. and other nations never been given any chance to vote directly on whether or not we want all these repressive new laws?

Why are few of us protesting the new security acts or demanding their repeal? Do we fear making waves? Do we think these laws will never apply to us? Recall what the German pastor Martin Niemöller wrote about the Nazis after his arrest in 1937. "First they came for the communists, and I did not speak out, because I was not a communist; then they came for the socialists, and I did not speak out, because I was not a socialist; then they came for the trade unionists, and I did not speak out, because I was not a trade unionist; then they came for the Jews, and I did not speak out, because I was not a Jew; then they came for me, and there was no one left to speak out for me."

Beware when a government can punish those who disagree. Like the Alien and Sedition Acts passed in 1798 by President John Adams and the Federalists to repress wide support for Thomas Jefferson, the Patriot Acts blur the lines between illegal acts of violent terrorism and legal acts of peaceful dissent. After 9/11, the White House press secretary told reporters, "Watch what you say." Today the president wants to bar the press from reporting his illegal actions. The Big Chill is on. We suffer from fake debate in the marketplace of ideas.

We need dissent, but only nonviolent dissent will do. Even verbal violence in the name of peace is self defeating. In writing this chapter, for example, I've struggled to tone down the sarcasm in Paine's essay. While I can't hide my resentment at the loss of our rights, I must urge a *peaceful* response. Spilling a single drop of blood by our own hand is too high a price if it means the loss of our souls.

RECONCILIATION with tyranny in any form is a dangerous doctrine. If we foolishly resign ourselves to a loss of our freedom in trade for a hope of security, the entire strength of the leaders in charge will be exerted to keep dissent as silent or invisible as possible.

Individuals are mere space debris in the orbit of regal politicians. Our masters consider our good no more than it serves their purposes. Their self interest leads them to suppress our freedom and silence our voices in each case that does not serve their purposes. They will leave us alone only if we do not interfere with them. When our protests are too noisy, they will do all in their power to put us down.

Even in constitutional republics, if we accept the reactionary new security laws as moral, if we agree to end our protests, what will stop our leaders from tapping our telephones? What will stop them from planting spies in our peaceful meetings? What will stop them from staging midnight "Palmer raids" to arrest the dissenters?

Despotic governments hate the lovers of peace and freedom. Such regimes cannot stay long at rest, for they are always fighting real and imagined enemies, foreign and domestic. Each act of disrespect and defiance provokes from them another round of retribution.

LET'S look at worst case and best case scenarios.

Worst case scenario: America tries to become a new global Roman Empire. The president in 2002 decreed world military superiority, the right to wage preemptive war without any authorization by the United Nations. As the U.S. invasions of Afghanistan and Iraq prove, this has meant ignoring the Geneva Conventions abroad and a loss of liberties at home. The trends are ominous. Democracy itself is at risk.

On September 11, 2001, the president declared a state of national emergency that's still in effect. What if America suffers more terrorist attacks, if we endure more natural disasters like Hurricane Katrina, if the economy fails or race riots erupt? As Commander in Chief, could the president declare martial law? Impossible? Nothing is impossible. Improbable? Mary Wollstonecraft warned us, "Every political good carried to the extreme must be productive of evil."

For a scary cautionary tale, read the 1935 novel by Sinclair Lewis, *It Can't Happen Here*. A populist fascist (akin to Huey Long) wins the 1936 presidential election. He declares a state of emergency to fight the Depression, censors the press, suspends elections, and turns sports stadiums into prison camps for dissenters. Could such a disaster ever befall America? Voltaire warned us, "It is dangerous to be right when the government is wrong."

Far worse would be if America continues its path of forcing regime changes in countries that are unfriendly to U.S. commercial interests. Stephen Kinzer's *Overthrow* reports 14 times since 1898 the U.S. has dislodged governments with invasions or coups, each time planting the seeds of future conflict. Overturning Iran's elected government in 1953 and installing the Shah to serve U.S. and British oil interests, for instance, not only erased actual democracy in the region, it provoked distrust and resentment that erupted in Iran's 1979 Islamic revolution. The West itself incited those fundamentalist forces today preventing world peace. So, my worst case scenario is that our selfish, myopic actions will keep fueling endless war on earth.

Best case scenario: Our leaders see the political and humanitarian value of raining seeds, blankets, medicines, and books on rebellious people instead of bombs. We use diplomacy and prosperity to shift vengeful enemies into heartfelt friends. Impossible? Improbable?

As a sign of hope, after the 2004 Indian Ocean tsunami that killed 200,000 people from 50 nations, a global disaster relief effort proved that together we *can* promote peaceful cooperation.

Additionally, we can vote corrupt leaders out of office. The U.S. elections in 2006 and 2008 are pivotal. Elections in every nation are crucial now. We decide the future by voting on election day, or by not voting at all. When all the votes are tallied, will we see horror or hope winning at the polls? Will we vote to renew democracy or to abandon it? My best case scenario is that democracy works.

Yet remember what Paine told colonial Americans.

> It is scarcely worth our while to fight against a con-
> temptible ministry only. Dearly, dearly, do we pay for the
> repeal of the [intolerable] acts, if that is all we fight for.

Amending or repealing laws like the Patriot Acts are not enough. We need to work for a world free of all authoritarian governments. We need a global vision to guide us. We need to unite personal growth and politics. *Liberating ourselves liberates our world.*

That government is best which governs the least,
because its people discipline themselves.
— THOMAS JEFFERSON

6. Genuine Democracy

KINGS and other masters can hold onto power only when enough of us consent to obey them. What if more of us release our craving to rule or be ruled? Could we mature into genuine democracy?

Cynicism about direct democracy is unfair and a deceit, because such an open government has never been tried in any modern nation. Our experiments in freedom have not yet been so bold.

Democracy on earth is far from perfect, but praise the progress we have made so far. We've come a long way. The progress resulted from our growth as human beings. This is why the governments in the U.S. and other democracies have not been as oppressive as in the nations ruled by absolute kings, dictators or warlords. Paine said it plainly:

> Laying aside all national pride and prejudice in favor of modes and forms, the plain truth is, that [the ascent of liberty] is wholly owing to the constitution of the people, and not to the constitution of the government.

Do we want to live within nations where the people instead of the government have the final say? We now get an indirect vote on laws by electing lawmakers. What if those we elect instead must draft laws for our ratification? Instead of a signature by the president enacting laws, what if a vote by the people is required to enact our new laws? *Are we ready for government by the consent of the governed?*

The good news is that the elements for real democracy are falling into place. Already we're guiding leaders with public opinion polling. Already diverse legislatures place referendums on ballots for voters' approval. Already grassroots initiatives (despite corruptions) allow us to bypass legislatures entirely and appeal directly to our fellow voters. Further, the Internet could let us vote on any proposed law, whether from a national legislature or a town council. Why not build on these advances to make true democracy a way of life?

There are risks on the path to direct democracy. What can prevent the government from manipulating public opinion in collusion with mass media? Also, what can prevent leaders from perpetrating online vote fraud? More primal, more perilous, is Internet voting technology too far ahead of our capacity to use it wisely?

If we want to enjoy genuine democracy someday, let's work for it now. Evolving the necessary maturity may take many generations to achieve. I've been working on my own growth for decades, and I still have a long way to go. Yet given the progress I've seen within myself, I'm convinced that humanity can and will mature enough so that one day a global network of open democracies can and will emerge.

More good news is that a global enlightenment movement already is teaching us that we're all interconnected. This awareness is causing us to think about the local to global consequences of our choices. As a result, more of us on earth are starting to practice mindful self rule and personal democracy, even unwittingly. This offers hope.

The spiritual power for moral self determination already dwells within us all. Why delay the dawning of global consciousness when we'll heal our childhood traumas and learn how to live in peace? If the separate fingers of one hand can work together, if individuals can live together in a peaceful community, so can nations.

Realize any vision with realism. Let's begin by getting clear about our compulsive need to be ruled by kings and other masters. Here is how Paine raised the subject at the end of Part I in *Common Sense.*

> For as we are never in a proper condition of doing justice to others, while we continue under the influence of some leading partiality, so neither are we capable of doing it to ourselves while we remain fettered by any obstinate prejudice. And as a man, who is attached to a prostitute, is unfitted to choose or judge of a wife, so any prepossession [or bias] in favor of a rotten constitution of government will disable us from discerning a good one.

II. Male Rule and Authority Addiction

All men would be tyrants if they could.
                                    – ABIGAIL ADAMS

7. The Divine Right of Kings

MY FATHER was a good man who gave up on his dreams.

Born 1920 in Chicago, he took art classes in youth at Jane Addams Hull House while dreaming of a career as a painter and art teacher. He earned a teaching degree from Northwestern in 1941, then enlisted in the U.S. Army. Posted as a photography instructor at Lowry Air Field in Denver, his secret job was producing a training film for the Norden bombsight, used with lethal skill over Germany and Japan.

While at Lowry, he met my mother at a party for Jewish youth in the base chapel. She invited the soldier home for Passover sedar. He sat down at my grandmother's dinner table, goes the family story, and never left. My mother's salesman father, however, declared that no "underpaid school teacher" could marry his daughter.

At the end of World War II, my father found a graphics job with a Denver printer and married my mother. He eventually opened his own advertising and public relations agency. When his business failed in 1965, he found a job as the marketing executive for a regional house paint manufacturer and retailer. He spent the next 20 years producing the same newspaper ad each week. In his time off, he took our family camping and volunteered for community organizations.

My father retired in 1985. He spent the last years of his life touring the world with my mother, taking nature photographs, then coming home to paint exquisite watercolors from his photos. I once asked him in a vulnerable moment why he never went after a career as an artist. He replied, "I wasn't good enough." He was mistaken.

The truth is that this man of talent and public service sacrificed his creative ambitions to become a husband and father. He projected his unfulfilled dreams onto me as his only son. When I was a child and adolescent, he took out his frustrations on me. A fear of his explosive anger and abuse left me with little self worth while implanting in me a resentment of authority that plagued me well into adulthood.

My father and I worked on our relationship before he died in 2000. I confronted his habit when we met of always asking, "Is everything under control?" He never asked, "How do you feel?"

On the night of his death, as I was leaving his hospice bed, in his eyes glowed the wordless light of unconditional love that I'd wanted from him for my entire life. That moment healed me.

Looking back at my father and my reactions to him, I've come to doubt presumptions that men must control everything or that being a man means going to war. As global thinking has prompted growing awareness of our planetary power, I've come to join with Tom Paine in disputing the "divine right" of kings to rule our world.

In Part II of *Common Sense,* Paine cited monarchy and hereditary succession as obstacles to democracy. I'll update his views by naming *alpha male rule* and *authority addiction* as deeper barriers.

> **HUMANKIND** "being originally equals in the order of creation, the equality could only be destroyed by some subsequent circumstance; the distinctions of rich, and poor, may in a great measure be accounted for.... But there is another and greater distinction for which no truly natural or religious reason can be assigned, and that is, the distinction of men into KINGS and SUBJECTS.
>
> Male and female are the distinctions of nature, good and bad the distinctions of heaven; but how a race of men came into the world so exalted above the rest, and distinguished like some new species, is worth enquiring into, and whether they [who claim to be our kings] are the means of happiness or of misery to [hu]mankind.

A king ruled by law was a major step ahead in human progress, but constitutions don't restrain all monarchs on earth, as in Saudi Arabia. In the best cases, a "benign despot" may lead us sagely, but for every good monarch, there are many others who are not so good.

In periods of disorder, charismatic leaders arise and attract ardent True Believers. They use force and fraud to inflict their law and order. If we consent to their moral authority over us, we must surrender our freedom of conscience. We must learn to be silent in a culture where unquestioning obedience is hailed as a civic virtue.

A dictatorship is contrary to human nature. If each of us is created equal with inalienable natural rights and duties, if we each are aspects of God, then no leaders or groups (whether in a position of authority by accident of birth or ascent by merit) have a right to put their family or friends in perpetual power and exclude all others from leadership. *No one has a natural right to pass power to their kin.*

The benevolent despot of the hour may deserve honor, but as Paine saw with mad King George III, the son of any monarch may descend into folly. Our leadership habits too often lack logic or decency. Why? Let's study fact and myth to learn why we idolize our leaders.

AT THIS point, Paine treats us to a biblical history lesson.

> In the early ages of the world, according to the scripture chronology, there were no kings; the consequence of which was, there were no wars; it is the pride of kings which throw mankind into confusion.... The first patriarchs' [lives] hath a happy something in them, which vanishes away when we come to the history of Jewish royalty.

The lineage of King David, seen as the bloodline of the messiah, has influenced the religions of Judaism, Christianity and Islam. Paine focused on how the Israelites wanted a king after conquering Canaan, but let's start in the beginning of the biblical "his-story."

The mythical "first" man and woman have different names and tribal tales in different lands. In the Bible, they are Adam and Eve.* Likely out of Africa, perhaps they lived in the Tigris-Euphrates valley (now Iraq), a garden where agriculture began 10,000 years ago.

According to Riane Eisler's *The Chalice and the Blade*, since only women can give birth, matriarchs ruled neolithic Mesopotamia. Tribal lineage was traced from mothers to daughters. People worshiped the feminine fertility principle, the creative goddess energy called Inanna or Ishtar, the lifeforce that causes fruit to appear on a tree.

May I propose a theory? One day as some impassioned woman felt tempted by her man's rising serpent, this archetypal Eve shared with her archetypal Adam the Fruit of the Tree of Knowledge. She told him of women marking sex days on their moon calendars. She told him the secret of the "holy hole." She admitted sex creates babies.

---

* Some believe Adam had a prior wife, Lilith, who was too independent for him.

Adam now realized his joyjuice was not so pointless. He realized that women had held onto tribal power by withholding the truth about sex. Adam felt cheated. He felt furious. He felt shafted. His reaction? Adam told other men, and these men seized power.

Is it possible men once were ignorant of their role in procreation? Support for the theory of men not knowing about their own fertility comes from the *Mabinogeon*, the book of Celtic mythology. In that lore, the Old Tribes were ruled by women who'd kept hidden the truth about male potency. The New Tribes were ruled by the men, who had learned the truth and felt betrayed after generations of female power. The Old Tribes fell as the New Tribes arose.

Vengeful after lifetimes of submission under matriarchal authority, the Celtic men imposed patriarchy. The lineage now would be traced from fathers to sons. The only way to assure the paternity of every son was to control every woman's womb, so men invented wedlock. They claimed ownership of their wives as private property. Children born outside of marriage were rejected as bastards.

When the men took over human society, a male godhead replaced the female goddess. Intellect replaced emotion. Lust replaced love. Perfectionism replaced compassion. Private property laws replaced generous sharing. Hierarchy replaced equality. Competition replaced cooperation. War replaced peace. Indeed, as Paine wrote, the palaces of kings *are* built on the ruins of the bowers of paradise.

Is this what occurred in mythic Eden after men learned the facts of life? Where once the bed was the home for sweet and sweaty ecstasy (long and slow and deep), did the bedroom become a war zone in the battle of the sexes? Twisted by a lust for power, did healthy sexuality became forbidden, dirty, sinful? Was this the origin of *original sin*? Was the "Fall of Man" really the Rise of Male Rule?

If so, then we humans are *not* innately evil, after all. If no original sin stains our souls, we do not need a messiah to save us. By knowing God within, we no longer need any alpha male to rule us.

IS MALE dominance a genetic trait for us humans? Women have maternal instincts. Do men have patriarchal instincts?

An alpha male chimpanzee may kill other males competing for his harem. Yet the peaceful bonobo chimps are egalitarian or matriarchal, choosing to make love not war. Both primates clearly understand sex and power. Who gave the *fruit of knowledge* to these chimps? Both chimps are 98 percent genetically identical to us humans. Are humans more akin to the violent or the peaceful primates?

Whatever you believe about human origins, once men grasped the fertile power of sex, I suggest, male rule became moral law.

Human civilization has been guided by a map of reality that makes sense of life and evolution as a male war for dominance, the survival of the fittest, since might makes right. This vision of life, lately called "Social Darwinism," has caused much suffering on earth.

Let's be clear about Charles Darwin's study on "natural selection." Many claim that a willingness to lie, cheat, bully, or kill means we are the most fit to survive. *The Origin of Species* instead reports that the "fittest" are the ones who can best meet life's changing conditions by *adaptation* to new circumstances. The "survival of the fittest" really means adapting in the right way. In truth, *right makes might.*

Despite cultural variations worldwide, the social contract that men and women inherit is a bum bargain for us both. According to Warren Farrell in *Why Men Are the Way They Are*, the man agrees to be the best at something to prove he can reliably provide "home, family and security" for a beautiful and faithful wife. She pledges sexual fidelity with a promise to be modest in public yet wanton in bed; in trade, she gets security. The man becomes a walking wallet for the woman, but he must prove to her his valor or value in real or symbolic combat. The system requires men to fight each other over women.

Do you feel men got the better side of the barter? Herb Goldberg in *The Hazards of Being Male* and Warren Farrell in *The Myth of Male Power* report that men pay for being in charge by early deaths from wars, dangerous jobs, high stress, and inner conflicts. Worse, by believing that manhood is measured by muscles or intellect, to be a "real man," most of us men live blocked off from our own emotions, secretly ruled by our shame, cut off from our hearts and our souls, spiritually castrated, which is no life at all. Hiding behind pretensions, we're like Ralph Ellison's invisible man in a superhero mask.

JUMP from Adam to Abraham. About 2000 BCE, Abraham freed his mind from the worldview of polytheism, worshiping every form of life as a distinct god. He realized all life expresses only One God. Monotheism was an evolutionary spiritual breakthrough.

Then called Abram, this Chaldean nomad from Ur (in Iraq), heard God promise that his male seed would rule all the Iron Age lands he'd traveled from the Tigris-Euphrates to the Nile (Genesis 15:18). Once called the Fertile Crescent, all of this was his "promised land."

After decades without a child, Abraham's barren wife Sarah, then called Sarai, placed her aging husband's hand into the hand of Hagar, her Egyptian slave. Skittish Hagar skedaddled. However, an angel in the desert promised that her son would sire a nation. Pregnant Hagar returned and bore Ishmael, who was circumcised as Abraham's heir. Sarah, as promised, treated Hagar's bastard boy as her own.

Ten years after, Abraham migrated into the Negev desert, a region of dry hills in the southern half of Israel today. In the Kadesh court, Abraham presented his wife as his sister, as he'd done before in the Egyptian court. As in Egypt, the ruler called still-alluring Sarah to his bed, as any king had the right to do. Abraham chose to be the cuckold to avoid being murdered as an obstacle. As in Egypt, God warned the ruler in a dream that Abraham was the husband.

Note what Abraham told the king. Admitting he had feared for his life, Abraham added (Gen. 20:12), "Besides she is indeed my sister, the daughter of my father but not the daughter of my mother; and she became my wife." What? *Abraham wed his half-sister?*

To be sure, I checked other versions of the Bible. I even asked a Greek Orthodox scholar to translate the surviving Septuagint source text.* Same statement. Was Abe telling the truth? His life was safe, and the king had promised free land as an apology, so why lie?

After he'd turned 99, Abraham told his wife that God had renewed the pledge he would father a nation by her. Post-menopausal Sarah laughed at him; then she conceived and bore a son. Abraham kept his covenant with God, circumcising the boy, naming him Isaac.

If Abraham did marry a paternal half-sister, then Isaac was a child of incest. Inbreeding later was outlawed in *Leviticus*, but it was not yet a taboo, for Isaac married his first cousin, Rebecca. We can fairly ask, was Isaac's bloodline tainted with DNA flaws passing from him to Jacob and on down to David, maybe down to Jesus? Is the glorious primogeniture of Judaic monarchy not so glorious?

---

*The Hebrew scrolls were lost in the 70 CE destruction of the 2nd Temple. The Greek translation that survived was not translated back into Hebrew until the 9th century. All these translations call into question the reliability of the English text. (I'm quoting a Revised Standard version, not the King James Bible of Paine's day.)

Fact or myth, we now have one Patriarch fathering two sons by two mothers. Abraham begat Ishmael by Hagar, then Isaac by Sarah. When Isaac was age ten, jealous Sarah told Abraham (Gen. 21:10), "Cast out this slave woman with her son, for the son of this slave woman shall not be heir with my son Isaac."

Abraham then exiled Hagar and Ishmael to wander in the desert, but only after God vowed that his beloved first son also would grow to father a nation. Both brothers shared the covenant with God, who promised land to both of Abraham's sons. Did God promise the same land? Has Western civilization been at war for thousands of years in a family feud over the inherited title to a misbegotten throne?

LEAP centuries ahead to when the Jews first asked for a king.

Ishmael's daughter, Mahalath, married Isaac's eldest son, Esau, who was tricked by younger brother Jacob into selling the birthright. Ishmael's heirs felt twice cheated out of Abraham's legacy.

Jacob wrestled with an angel and was renamed Israel. One of his 12 sons, Joseph, was sold into slavery in Egypt. He rose to power and brought his family to Egypt, where they were fruitful and multiplied exceedingly. Joseph died and enslavement followed. His descendant, Moses, led the Israelites out of bondage. After receiving The Law at Mt. Sinai, they held a social contract: God would give them the land promised to Abraham in trade for obeying the Law of Moses.

The Israelites then invaded Canaan. By about 1200 BCE, they had conquered the Ishmaelites, displacing their kin. Judges in Sanhedrin assemblies used the law of the Torah to govern the 12 tribes of Israel, which became the world's *first* republic. (An assembly of elders had existed centuries earlier in Sumeria, but a king ruled that appointed body, so it was not a republic like Israel.) Democracy did not arise again on the planet until about 500 BCE in Athens.

Surrounded by foes, as the only people ruled by laws not kings, the Israelites likely felt inferior. Once a powerful pharaoh had protected them; now they felt afraid. After a victory, men came to the mighty warrior Gideon and demanded (Judges 8:22), "Rule over us, you and your son and his grandson also; for you have delivered us out of the hands of the Medianites." But Gideon replied to them, "I will not rule over you, and my son will not rule over you; the Lord will rule over you." Commenting on this, Paine said that until the ancient Israelites under a national delusion requested a king, [Israel] was a kind of republic administered by a judge and the elders of the tribes. Kings they had none, and it was held sinful to acknowledge any being under that title but the Lord of Hosts.... Gideon doth not decline the honor [of a king] but denieth their right to give it; neither doth he compliment them with invented declarations of his thanks, but in the positive style of a prophet charges them with disaffection to their proper sovereign, the King of Heaven.

PAINE next hopped ahead to about 1000 BCE. The aging prophet Samuel had named his two sons as judges over Israel (I Samuel 8:4). Citing sins by the wayward lads, tribal elders went to the prophet and said, "Behold you are old and your sons do not walk in your ways, now appoint for us a king to judge us like all the other nations."

The demand displeased Samuel, who like Gideon felt God should rule though the Torah. He prayed. God said, "Hearken to the voice of the people in all that they say to you, for they have not rejected you, but they have rejected me from being king over them."

Samuel did not trust the people, so he staged a rigged lottery. The lot fell to tall Saul, who stood head and shoulders above all the rest. Samuel anointed the handsome man, but Saul failed as the king from dark moods and dark deeds. Samuel withdrew his support and instead anointed David the giant killer, the shepherd who'd slain Goliath the Philistine. By crowning David—a descendant of Abraham, Isaac and Jacob—Samuel affirmed that bloodline's divine right to rule.

After defeating Saul in a civil war, David sired Solomon, who built the Temple. After Solomon died, his sons' turf war split the kingdom into Israel in the north and Judah in the south.

Sargon of Assyria (Syria) in 722 BC enslaved Israel, marching its ten tribes north, where they vanished. Where they lost to genocide? Assyria was conquered by Nebuchadnezzar, whose vast Babylonian-Chaldean empire stretched from the Tigris-Euphrates to the Nile (the "promised land"). The Babylonians occupied Judah in 604 BCE.

Having abandoned a republic for a kingdom, the Judeans now lost their national independence. Repeated Judean revolts infuriated the Babylonians, who destroyed Solomon's Temple in 586 BCE, exiling the two surviving Judean tribes to Babylon (Iraq).

In Babylon, the Judeans absorbed apocalyptic Zoroastrian myths of a warrior Savior defeating a Devil in a final battle. *The concept of a messiah had never before existed in Jewish theology.* Nothing in the five books of Moses predicted a messiah. The Zoroastrian-influenced books written at that time, like Ezekiel and Second Isaiah, would later became favorites of Jews and Christians alike. However, the wish for a savior or a messiah is contrary to natural Judaism.

Babylon was conquered by Persia (Iran) in 539 BCE. Victorious Darius I let the Judeans return to Jerusalem after 70 years of exile to rebuild the Temple in Palestine (i.e., Philistine, formerly Phoenicia). The heirs of Isaac again ousted the heirs of Ishmael.

Persian rule gave way to Greek occupation when Alexander the Great defeated Darius III in 333 BCE. After Alexander died in 323, Ptolemy's Egypt ruled Judea until Syrian Greeks usurped control. The Maccabean revolt in 167-64 BCE restored Judean independence with support from Rome, which later supplied troops to resolve a civil war between lower class Pharisees and aristocratic Sadducees. By 63 BCE Palestine had become a province of Rome, which halted troublesome Judean nationalism in 70 CE by destroying the rebuilt second temple. Sarah's children scattered. Hagar's children reclaimed the land.

The Jewish diaspora ended in 1948 when the state of Israel was reborn under a mandate from the United Nations. The UN offered a state to the Palestinians, who rejected the offer, denying the right of Israel to exist again. Perpetuating the ancient bloodfeud of brothers Isaac and Ishmael, Jews and Arabs today are invested in one another's collective guilt. Will it all end in a battle at Armageddon?

Citing the Holy Scriptures as proof, Paine rejected the divine right of kings. He asserted that the Jewish experiment in royalty had failed (that is, it *plotzed*). Why? God's way is democracy, not monarchy.

> The will of the Almighty, as declared by Gideon and the prophet Samuel, expressly disapproves of government by kings. All anti-monarchial parts of scripture have been very smoothly glossed over.... These portions of scripture are direct and positive. They admit no equivocal construction. That the Almighty hath here entered his protest against monarchial government is true, or the scripture is false.

It is not birth but virtue
that makes the difference.
— VOLTAIRE

8. Hereditary Succession

AFTER arguing that the "divine right" of kings is *not* God's will, Thomas Paine disputed kings passing power down to their sons. We can learn from his arguments by thinking about how we still tend to support hereditary rights in our modern world.

> To the [social] evil of monarchy we have added that of hereditary succession, and as the first is a degradation and lessening of ourselves, so the second, claimed as a matter of right, is an insult and an imposition on posterity.
>
> For all men [and women] being originally equals, no one by birth could have a right to set up his own family in perpetual preference to all others for ever.... It is one of those evils, which when once established is not easily removed.... One of the strongest natural proofs of the folly of hereditary right in kings, is, that nature disapproves it, otherwise she would not so frequently turn it into ridicule by giving [hu]mankind an ass for a lion.

By this quip he means, giving us a bad king instead of a good one.

> This is supposing the present race of kings in the world to have had an honorable origin; whereas it is more than probable, that... the first [king in a line was] nothing better than the principal ruffian of some restless gang, whose savage manners or preeminence in subtlety obtained him the title of chief among plunderers. [Hail to the thief!]
>
> However, it is needless to spend much time in exposing the folly of hereditary right. If there are any so weak as to believe it, let them promiscuously worship the ass and lion, and welcome. I shall neither copy [their folly], nor disturb their devotion.

Too bad Paine stopped there. He was onto something important. We need to know why we humans tend to "promiscuously worship" our leaders. We will get to that shortly, but first let's follow Paine's inquiry into the origin of hereditary kings.

> Yet I should be glad to ask how they [the worshipers of hereditary rights] suppose kings came at first? The question admits but of three answers, *viz,* either by lot, by election, or by usurpation.

Let's join Thomas Paine to consider each option in turn as a basis for discussion. Our discourse may shed light on today's problems.

> **IF THE** first king was taken by lot, it establishes a precedent for the next [king being chosen by lottery], which excludes hereditary succession. Saul was by lot, yet the succession was not hereditary, neither does it appear from the transaction there was any intention it ever should, for the 'divine right' to royal lineage was given to David, which is why Jesus was supposed to be the king of the Jews.

In the spirit of Paine, let's now think critically about the hereditary right to rule of a tiny Jesus the zygote, of whom acolytes abound.

The book of Matthew traces Jesus' bloodline through his mother's betrothed, Joseph, back to David, Abraham and Adam. But Mary's "virgin birth" means the fetus in her womb lacked a human father. If "immaculate conception" really was the case, if Joseph was *not* the child's father, how could Jesus be a descendant of David?

An answer lay in Luke, which claimed Mary also was descended from David. Whether true or not, the point for us here is that Jesus' "divine right" to rule traces back to an alpha male king.

We need to recall that Christianity chiefly was propagated outside Palestine among non-Jews in the Roman Empire. These were male-dominated Hellenistic societies rife with Adonis resurrection myths and lusty he-man gods loping around impregnating virgins for sport. How much were the Gospels tailored to fit these audiences?

With respect for all those who love Jesus, in the cause of reason, we must ask, did the title "King of Kings" have more to do with savvy marketing than any legal right of Jesus to the Judean throne?

Are the Old and New Testaments like a pair of twin nuts bolting together Western Civilization to anchor alpha male rule? The Lord's Prayer, I believe, feels so comforting precisely because it reinforces our undemocratic, paternalistic codependence on kings. "Our Father who art in Heaven... Thy Kingdom come." Why see God as a king up and away from us? Isn't that how we see government?

Whether or not the Resurrection happened, reason tells us that the popularity of early Christianity partly came from joining spirituality and politics. Please recall the story of Jesus and the money changers, the incident justifying his arrest during Passover. The Temple allowed worshipers to sacrifice at the altar only pure white birds, likely doves, say scholars. These pure birds could be bought only with pure coins, sold only by money changers at the Temple entrance. Guards drove away the poor, all those who could not pay to pray.

Denouncing the Temple as "a den of thieves," Jesus overturned the tables of the money changers. With his outburst of civil disobedience, Jesus protested selling access to God (just as Martin Luther would do 1,500 years later). Jesus declared that God is not for sale. He declared that God is free to anyone, anywhere, anytime.

Rather than knowing God indirectly through an intermediary, as in a monarchy, I believe Jesus called for knowing God directly, as in a democracy. Warning us not to look to the sky for salvation, Jesus said the kingdom of God is within us all. Have we missed his redeeming message of self liberation for 2,000 years? Has humanity been so busy worshiping King Jesus as our drug-of-choice that we've turned a martyred spiritual evolutionary into an opiate of the masses?

Applying the Gospel to our modern times, as Christian evangelical Jim Wallis attests in *God's Politics*, Jesus would condemn those who hold aloft a Bible to preach intolerance and war. Jesus told us to love and forgive our enemies. He said, "Blessed are the peacemakers."

ANOINTED a king by lot, Saul was usurped by David, who sired the royal lineage supposedly inherited by Jesus. To find a ruler who was elected, study the choice of Mohammed's successor.

Born near Mecca around 570 CE, called by some a descendant of Abraham and Ishmael, Mohammed received his first visions at age 40 in a cave near Mecca. He saw that he was the last Judaic prophet, the successor of Jesus. His visions form the Koran (*Qur'an*).

Arising amid polytheism, Islam has five pillars of faith: Bearing witness to the One and Only God, Allah *(Shahadatain)*; praying five times daily while kneeling toward Mecca *(Salah)*; a social welfare tax *(Zakkah)*; fasting sunrise to sunset during holy month *(Ramadan)*; and once in life, if able, making a pilgrimage *(Hajj)* between Medina and Mecca in the path of the prophet Mohammed, who revered the personal struggle (*jihad)* for inner peace.

The death of Mohammed in 632 provoked a fight over succession to the throne of the Prophet. An early convert named Ali, husband of Mohammed's daughter, Fatima, advocated hereditary succession; and the Prophet's family backed his bid. But another disciple, Abu Bakr, was chosen the successor by a communal vote of the faithful.

The schism that erupted divides Islam still. Supporters of elected succession became the *Sunni* branch of Islam, comprising 85 percent of all Muslims today. The remainder of Islam is the *Shiite* sect, which adheres to male-line hereditary succession. Both segments of Islam tends to treat women as the men's property.

Most Islamic nations today are ruled by kings or dictators bent on dynastic legacies, as in Saudi Arabia, Jordan and Syria. Authoritarian men govern despite democratic aspirations by the moderate majority of Muslims, including the women who rarely get any vote at all.

Islam's majority Sunni tradition supports *electing* the Prophet's successor, so why not democratically elect civilian leaders from men and women in every Islamic land? Could real democracy end Islam's bloodfeuds with Judaism, Christianity and Hinduism? Is it heresy to observe that Mohammed taught peace, mercy and tolerance?

IF THE first king of any country was [chosen] by election, that likewise establishes a precedent for the next; for to say, that the right of all future generations [to vote] is taken away by the act of the first electors in their choice not only of a king, but of a family of kings for ever, hath no parallel in or out of scripture but the doctrine of original sin, which supposes the free will of all men lost in Adam; and from such comparison... hereditary succession can derive no glory.... Dishonorable rank! Inglorious connection! Yet the most subtle sophist cannot produce a juster simile.

Witness Paine's own sophistry here. When he wrote about original sin, please realize that he was a deist writing for Christians.

Those who profess the idea of God in *deism*, then and now, assert that God and God's natural laws can be learned only though reason from observations of nature. Deists reject blind faith in any revealed religion. Paine knew Christians believe we're all sinful from birth, so we need salvation. As a deist, though, he believed that we're naturally good from birth. We each express nature and nature's God. If all life is God, and if God is innately good, since we're alive, we are innately good, so we do not need a savior. This was Paine's deist logic.

Like Paine, most of the founders of the United States were deists, *not* Christians. Most of them were freethinking freemasons, such as Franklin, Jefferson and Washington, who as the first president signed the Treaty of Tripoli that said, "The government of the United States is not, in any sense, founded on the Christian religion."

Do not be fooled by propaganda claiming America always was a Christian nation. The first pilgrim colonists on the Mayflower in 1620 did include Christian Puritans fleeing England, but their dogmatism did not inspire America's revolution. Indeed, the deist founders of the U.S. would feel appalled to hear their names cited to justify religious intolerance or an end to the separation of church and state.

Deism influenced the Unitarian faith and later Transcendentalism, a 19th century movement led by Ralph Waldo Emerson (*Nature, Self Reliance)* and Henry David Thoreau (*Walden, Civil Disobedience*). Transcendentalism sprouted beliefs that branched into *New Thought* denominations like Christian Science, Religious Science, Unity, and the Course in Miracles. Transcendentalism also bore fruit in the 20th century movements for equal rights led by Mahatma Gandhi and by Martin Luther King. Did you know deism had crafted our world?

Returning to my point, was Paine a hypocrite for citing scriptures in which he did not believe? Or was he voicing radical ideas in terms familiar to his readers, so they'd understand? Decide for yourself.

AS TO usurpation, no man will be so [fool]hardy as to defend it; and that William the Conqueror was an usurper is a fact not to be contradicted.... A French bastard landing [in 1066 CE] with an armed banditti, and establishing himself against the consent of the natives, is in plain terms a very paltry rascally origin.... The plain truth is, that the antiquity of English monarchy will not bear looking into.

But it is not so much the absurdity as the [social] evil of hereditary succession which concerns [hu]mankind. Did it ensure a race of good and wise men [to rule us], it would have the seal of divine authority, but as it opens a door to the foolish, the wicked, and the improper, it hath in it the nature of oppression. Men who look upon themselves [as] born to reign, and others to obey, soon grow insolent... and when they succeed to the [head of] government are frequently the most ignorant and unfit of any throughout the dominions.

In Britain today, almost a millennium since the Norman Conquest led to the current royal bloodline on the British throne, monarchs lack the political power once wielded by King George III. They mostly are figureheads, beloved by some, reviled by others.

Critics of the British monarchy, citing scandal after scandal, claim "the royals" do not deserve their lavish titles and wealth in trade for their comparatively minor ceremonial and philanthropic duties.

Some critics go further to oppose all hereditary kings and queens. They propose the abolition of the monarchy in Britain and every other land on earth. Whether the first king in a line was crowned by lottery, by election or by seizing power, they feel humanity at last is ready to be done with kings and other masters. Thomas Paine counted himself in that camp; I humbly join him. If we would declare our individual sovereignty and learn to live without kings, not only will our personal power to manage our lives increase, our children's children's children will inherit a better world.

In short, monarchy and succession have laid not this or that kingdom only, but the world in blood and ashes. 'Tis a form of government which the word of God bears testimony against, and blood will attend it....

The nearer any government approaches to a republic, the less business there is for a king.... For it is the republican and not the monarchical part of the constitution [that we] glory in... and it is easy to see that when republican virtue fails, slavery ensues.

In England a king hath little more to do than to make war and give away places; which in plain terms, is to impoverish the nation and set it together by the ears. A pretty business indeed for a man to be allowed eight hundred thousand sterling a year, and worshiped into the bargain! Of more worth is one honest man [or woman] to society, and in the sight of God, than all the crowned ruffians that ever lived.

I do not wish them to have power
over men, but over themselves.
— MARY WOLLSTONECRAFT

9. Inherited Wealth

THE American Dream entices men to become rich and powerful, then pass their legacy to their sons. This did not occur in my case.

My great grandfather on my father's side, a Polish tailor named Tonoplitsky, who fled the pogroms in eastern Europe, left Ellis Island more than a century ago with the name of Freed. Family stories differ, but I prefer the tale that he chose the name for its meaning.

The tailor's son became a barber, moved to Chicago, joined the Masons, and married a woman above his station who claimed descent from Spanish sephardic aristocracy. She bore two sons and a daughter. The barber's most famous customer was Al Capone, who daily let my grandfather shave him with a straight razor at his throat.

My father told me the biggest survival lesson he ever learned as a boy. His barber father took him to Round Lake northwest of Chicago, rowed out to the middle, then ordered the boy to jump in the water with his clothes on, telling his son, "Sink or swim." He swam.

My mother's paternal grandfather was an Ukrainian merchant, Judah Eisen Laskowitz, later renamed Lasky. He opened a mercantile in the Colorado mining town of Kremmling. His wife bore five sons and a daughter before the family moved to Denver.

The eldest, my grandfather William, became a travelling tobacco salesman. His job helped feed the family during the Great Depression. Two of his brothers became wealthy. Phil Lasky founded KPIX, the first radio and TV stations in San Francisco. Moses Lasky founded a big San Francisco law firm, personally pleading antitrust cases before the U.S. Supreme Court, living on Twin Peaks in a house designed for him by IM Pei. That generation of Laskys is now deceased.

I inherited none of the fortune on my mother's side of the family. From my father's side of the family, I saw scant worldly inheritance. What I mostly inherited from my dad was low self esteem, an abiding love of nature and a strong social conscience.

WE HAVE confused the inheritance of high moral and spiritual values with the inheritance of vast wealth and high property values. Such confusion has distorted our views of nature and natural law, as Thomas Paine discussed in *Agrarian Justice*:

> Man did not make the earth, and though he had a natural right to occupy it, he had no right to locate as his property in perpetuity any part of it; neither did the Creator of the earth open a land-office [to issue] first title deeds.

Does inherited wealth give affluent people a right to rule society? Hereditary dynasties have controlled most of the world's property and power. In the Industrial Revolution, for instance, a few families in America and England owned the key industries. France generally has been ruled since *l'Ancien Régime* by the "two hundred families," the ruling class clique united by marriage and politics with aristocratic relations across Europe, the Americas and around the world.

The distinctions of "old money" and "new money" persist among the wealthy. Some limit friendships to families in the Social Register. Yet clout will out. High society, like business and government, honors the "Cynical Golden Rule"—the one with the gold rules.

How do you feel about the fact and fantasy of inherited wealth? Do you feel that having money makes you any better than people with less? If you're living simply or in debt, perhaps surviving with public assistance, are you any worse than those living large? Does our value come from what we own and owe, or who we are inside?

Too many born into mansions make the phrase "trust-fund baby" mean the same as "wasted human potential." How many of us use our prosperity for posterity? How many of us are victims of materialism, possessed by our possessions? Economic self sufficiency is laudable, but are we free souls or mere cogs in the mercantile machine?

Is money the root of all evil? No, but a compulsive obsession with money hurts our souls. *Affluenza* by John DeGraaf, David Wann and Thomas Naylor calls mass consumerism an unsustainable epidemic. General Motors heiress and psychologist Jessie H. O'Neill, publisher of Affluenza.com, warns us about "a dysfunctional relationship with money and wealth, or the pursuit of it."

Has vitalizing capitalism mutated into a virulent plague?

John Locke wrote, "Our incomes are like our shoes; if too small, they gall and pinch us; but if too large, they cause us to stumble and trip." Is this the reality behind *economic determinism?* Does money decide our fate rather than God or our own free will?

Edmund Burke remarked, "If we command our wealth, we shall be rich and free; if our wealth commands us, we are poor indeed."

TO PLACE these thoughts into context, we need to look afresh at the ideas of Adam Smith, who conceived modern capitalism.

In 1759, Adam Smith published *The Theory of Moral Sentiments.* Moral choices, he said, require an act of imagination. Put yourself in the shoes of the other person, then act as they would act. Promoting empathy, the Golden Rule, Smith called it "sympathy." Morality must be guided by sympathy, yet emotions must be ruled by reason.

Almost two decades later on March 9, 1776, three months after Tom Paine published *Common Sense,* Adam Smith published the first of his five volumes in *The Wealth of Nations.* Like a one-two punch, after Tom Paine's writing turned politics on its head, Adam Smith's writings turned economics on its head.

Since the 1500s, *mercantilism* had defined the wealth of nations in terms of gold bullion in state treasuries. The methods of earning gold were manufacturing and exporting merchandise, taxing imports and selling colonial natural resources or agricultural products. This is why Europeans plundered the Americas along with Africa and Asia.

Adam Smith instead said national wealth lay in the commerce of its people. He calculated national wealth as the value of all the goods the people in a country consume daily. The wealth of nations relies on the marketplace, Smith said, so consumption of goods is an economic necessity. Capitalism *is* consumerism. Consumer spending comprises two-thirds of the economy in the U.S. This is why, after 9/11, leaders exhorted us to go out and buy something.

Smith favored ending hereditary occupations, where sons did the same job as their fathers. As part of the shift, he proposed the division of labor in factories, an idea that gave rise to mass production and the assembly line. Sadly, Smith discounted the value of labor, which later would upset Karl Marx and others.

If we have the freedom to earn our bread as we wish, if no king commands the economy, how does the grain get to market?

In Smith's *laissez faire** economy, "Every man [or woman], as long as he does not violate the laws of justice, is left perfectly free to pursue his own interest his own way, and to bring both his industry and capital into competition with those of any other man or order of men." He added, "It is not from the benevolence of the butcher, the brewer, or the baker that we expect our dinner, but from their regard to their own interest." In Adam Smith's utopia, the "invisible hand" of *enlightened self interest*, guided by moral sympathy, would direct all commercial affairs, so everyone in society prospers.

Did you realize Smith was a social progressive? He wrote, "Civil government, so far as it is instituted for the security of property, is in reality instituted for the defense of the rich against the poor."

Adam Smith wanted to see wealth and power widely distributed throughout society. He favored small business and small government. He did *not* envision a nation of shopkeepers, as some contend, for he actively promoted manufacturing. If his true plan had been heeded, capitalist economies likely would not suffer from the boom and bust "business cycle" that Marx criticized so effectively.

Smith viewed all monopolies as enemies of free enterprise and fair markets. He saw trade associations as conspiracies for raising prices. He said unfair or fraudulent market practices deserve regulation for public safety. He supported sanctions against outlaw enterprises and rogue nations, including the use of force as a last resort.

Every corporation lacking sympathy violates the morality of Adam Smith. He'd decry the inhumane global techno-capitalism now being malpracticed in his name. At the dawn of the Industrial Age, he wrote, "The robot is going to lose. Not by much. But when the final score is tallied, flesh and blood is going to beat the damn monster."

Why is Adam Smith so misunderstood?

Unlike other civil thinkers who first mapped out their vision for an ideal world and then gave a compass to navigate their terrain, Adam Smith published his moral compass first, and only later did he offer a map for his imagined world. Society has misread his map because we have forgotten his compass. This is how we've lost our way.

A NATIVE American proverb says, "We do not inherit the earth from our ancestors, we borrow it from our children." Opponents of oligarchy and plutocracy call for the abolition of all inherited wealth,

---

* From the French, "allow to do."

so each generation must learn self sufficiency. They support estate taxes for redistributing wealth in society. They call for land reform, so property is divided fairly among us all. Do you agree?

When we look at the tradition of inherited wealth, we discover that today in the U.S. and in other nations, the "means of production" are owned by corporations more often than by families. Given the legal status of persons, corporations possess more rights than individuals. Corporations may buy and sell companies at will, deciding the fate of all employees. We permit this, but condemn as slavery the practice of selling people directly. The "wage slaves" and "salary slaves" clearly are treated better than those in actual slavery, but employers still seem to treat employees the way medieval lords treated their serfs.

Worse, deregulated corporations wield broad power over national governments. Concerns about this go way back to the founding of the American republic, as documented by Thom Hartmann in *Unequal Protection* and *What Would Jefferson Do?* Thomas Jefferson himself wrote, "I hope we shall crush in its birth the aristocracy of our monied corporations which dare already to challenge our government to a trial by strength, and bid defiance to the laws of our country."

Given the shrinking middle class, the widening gap between rich and poor, are we seeing the return of feudalism with corporations as the modern hereditary kings and nobility in our world? If so, Paine's sharp criticism of monarchy now applies to them.

Are all republics today so driven by private capital that the name of democracy no longer suits these governments? Indeed, given vast corruption, can they rightly be called republics?

EVERY man feels pressure to pass on the legacy of his father and forefathers, but we need to update that expectation.

In my case, neither my departed father, grandfathers, nor uncles left any sizable inheritance to me. My mother inherited my father's modest savings, and when she died in 2006, I inherited a part of what was left. In reality, my father's best legacy was his love. What I most needed to inherit from him and did not, however, was a positive sense of what it means to be a "real man" in today's world.

Imagine humanity 50,000 years ago, before the Agricultural Age, before the rise of matriarchy and before the rise of male rule. Society was more balanced in those hunter-gatherer societies, anthropologists suggest. Men and women likely had separate roles, for the men best fit the jobs of hunters and tribal defenders while only women can bear children, but neither gender mattered more to the tribe than the other. Consequently, I believe, the men felt free to be their real selves, to be emotionally authentic. Men did not hide their hearts.

In "primitive" tribal societies, boys traditionally have become men at adolescence through a sacred rite of initiation. But in the modern world, we men are never initiated into adult life beyond being told to go get a job. We receive no true training in what Robert Bly calls the "male mode of feeling." We rarely go down into the darkness of our hidden shadow selves and return into the light of rich self realization, what Joseph Campbell called the "warrior's journey." Reclaiming our inner gold is the true wealth that men deserve to inherit.

Instead, we modern men get contradictory messages. We should marry a virgin, for example, but we're expected to "become a man" by making sure no virgins are left in the world. And women say they want men to be sensitive or vulnerable, but if we cry in front of them, too often they call us "wimps." It's a no-win double bind.

Because men today do not inherit from our fathers a knowledge of how to express the full range of our emotions, or how to be personally powerful without being violent, because men *are* in charge of society, the world is being ripped apart by men's inner conflicts.

Instead of inheriting our rightful spiritual power, we men fixate on inheriting worldly power. We crave to be hereditary kings with sons. What we really need is for our souls to be the ruler of our lives. If our "inner king" governs our daily choices, especially if our conscience is guided by global sense, we can know peace in our hearts and souls, which empowers us to create peace in the world.

What blocks all people (men and women alike) from achieving the personal growth to live free responsibly? To answer, we must at last face the question of why we idolize our leaders.

Man is born free, and everywhere he is in chains.
— JEAN JACQUES ROUSSEAU

10. Authority Addiction

WHY do the habits of our hearts and minds compel so many of us to worship kings and other alpha male masters? Why do we trust them despite all the muted alarms in the back of our minds screaming at us to run for our lives? Why do we sacrifice liberty for security?

Tom Paine had keen insights into the psychology behind tyranny. Please recall his remark about passing crowns from fathers to sons.

> If there are any so weak as to believe it [the divine right
> of kings], let them promiscuously worship the ass and lion.

Why do we not care if a king is bad or good so long as he's a king? Is any king better than no king at all? Paine referred to a dependence that modern psychology labels as an "addiction." To coin a phrase, the central problem is *generational authority addiction,* an unhealthy relationship with power passing from generation to generation.

We're enculturated to believe a social meme that we're incapable of ruling ourselves responsibly. Each generation of parents teaches their children to believe that we're all too stupid or imperfect or too corrupted by original sin to be trusted with freedom. Living in an unfree world, distrusting our impulse control, we've been raised to think we need a king or master to tell us what to do and keep us safe. Our insecurity is why we give away our power to leaders.

Dysfunctional power habits rule us. While we act from habit every day, like how we walk or talk, we're looking here at the habits behind dictatorships. For sharp clarity, *The True Believer* by Eric Hoffer and *Escape from Freedom* by Erich Fromm tell how culturally entrained reliance upon authority enabled the rise of totalitarian states like Nazi Germany, Fascist Italy, Soviet Russia, or Communist China.

Most of us have consented to a social contract based on the power habits we learned from our parents and our peers. Our parents were shaped by their parents and peers, and so on back to mythic Eden.

Focus on the family. No matter how we describe human origins, any reasonable person can agree that our parents' genes and actions implanted in us our core personality habits. We are a blending of both nature and nurture, heredity *and* environment.

Authoritarian governments start in authoritarian homes. Like adult children of alcoholics inherit addictive traits that they pass on to their children, the childhoods of all dictators likely were scarred by shame, blame and abuse from their parents. A boy beaten by his father may become a bully or become the target of bullies (as I did). The roots of authority addiction lay in our earliest survival mechanisms.

In terms of neurobiology, a genetic trait or a life experience causes the hypothalamus in our brains to release protein peptides that form emotional connections in our neural network. Repetition reinforces these links. If parents often berate a child, this can implant self-hate reactions that may take years of therapy to overcome.

Embedded neural patterns lead to addiction. Scientists have found that if a living brain is displayed on a PET scanner, what's seen with the eyes now and what's recalled as memory flash *equally* across the visual cortex like lightning storms on earth as seen from space. When peptide-driven emotions from memory compel how we react to live experiences now, if we can't stop our reaction, that's an addiction. An example is the man who tries to seduce every pretty woman he meets, a trait that Patrick Carnes calls a sex addiction. In essence, addictions are how we avoid our memories of emotional pain.

FOR insights into the nature of authority addiction, let's study the term, *"codependency."* Author Stephen Covey asserts our personality development cycle from infancy to adulthood ideally would progress from *dependence* to *independence* to *interdependence*. We'd mature into Maslow's "self-actualized" individuals. If we get stuck between dependence and independence, that's codependence.

Codependency is the compulsive need either to have another take care of us *or* to be a caretaker of someone else. A codependent person is not autonomous and self sufficient. This is why Jefferson advised, "Never trouble another for what you can do for yourself."

An example of codependency is a cigarette smoker sitting in a bar with matches at his elbow while calling for a light from the bartender, who retorts, "Want me to smoke it for you, too?"

People in codependent relationships need the *external validation* and compliance of one another to feel secure. Each is the "enabler" of the other's harmful habits, such as buying the booze for an alcoholic. Either or both parties in the relationship feel they alone are the victim. Contemplate the futile absurdity in desperately hoping to feel secure by trying to please those who can never be pleased by anyone because they feel so displeased with themselves.

In *Facing Codependency*, author Pia Mellody identifies five major symptoms of codependency: Low self esteem with difficulty loving oneself; lack of healthy boundaries with difficulty protecting oneself; an inability to meet one's personal needs with difficulty in self care; confused self concept with difficulty disclosing personal information appropriately; lack of moderation in self expression with difficulty acting appropriately to our age and social circumstances.

Codependency author Melody Beattie defines more traits: Always feeling angry or hostile (a defense against fear, pain, sadness); making unreasonable threats to get our way; seeking to control or manipulate others; shifting blame away from ourselves onto others; playing the martyr to prey on others' pity; or trying to control all those around us because we feel so out of control inside ourselves. Codependents also get absorbed in others' problems, offering unwanted advice, insisting upon solving other people's problems for them. We can behold such toxic behaviors in governments as well as in individuals.

TRYING to meet our unmet childhood needs, we adopt whatever social roles help us to feel secure. Like actors in a play, we act out our scripted authority roles from childhood in every social setting. Our roles evolve as we evolve, but we stay within our range.

Transactional Analysis in psychology labels three abusive power roles—*persecutor, rescuer* and *victim*. The trio is locked in a "drama triangle." Persecutors need victims. Rescuers need victims. Victims need persecutors, so they can be rescued. All three roles are traps, and I can attest to how all three roles leave us drained.

Here are four other power roles common in authority addiction:

We may be a *leader* who feels safe only by being in total control, harming those we govern, wishing to be both feared and adored.

We may be a *follower* who feels safe only when obeying a leader, fearing to think for ourselves, too timid to be our own boss.

We may be a *rebel* who feels safe only when fighting authority or else causing an uproar, mistaking aggravated attention for love.

We may be a *hermit* who feels safe only by refusing to be a leader, follower or rebel, by isolating ourselves, trying to be invisible.

All these roles are natural, perhaps necessary in a healthy society. Problems occur when we become so obsessively attached to any role that we feel compelled to perform that role all the time, like always having to be the boss at home or at work. This is why addiction is a chronic disease of immature impulsivity and selfishness.

We rely on split perceptions to deny our authority addiction. In the Tarot is a card called "The Devil." A horned figure on a throne holds chains looped loosely around the necks of a man and woman. They could lift off the chains, but they stand in mute bondage. They can't even conceive of freedom. In the same way, we are all born free, but everywhere we are enslaved in chains of our own choosing.

HOW do I know about the problem of authority addiction?

Back in 1971, I was recruited in Denver by a spiritual community called the Unified Family, which followed the teachings of a Korean master. I liked the group's ideal of uniting humanity into one family, but in retrospect, I really joined because of the acceptance I felt from the group members. I desperately needed to feel so loved.

Within a year after I joined the Family, the founder came back to America and reorganized all the centers nationally under a new name, The Unification Church. I was told to drop out of school, quit my job, and devote my energies to recruiting new members and fundraising. I was in too deep emotionally to question my orders.

My devotion helped me rise in the church. After service on a bus team supporting 16 new centers from Detroit to New Orleans, I was appointed by the master, Sun Myung Moon, to start a center in West Virginia. My job was to win new members while seeking allies in the churches and local to state governments.

After five months of failure, never recruiting anyone and barely keeping the new center afloat financially, I was demoted and sent to Kentucky. For seven months I bounced between the church centers in Lexington and Louisville, growing increasingly restless. I kept failing to recruit any new members, so again I was demoted. I was sent to a "mobile fundraising team" selling flowers on street corners.

Unhappy with my plight, wanting to raise my status in the church, I tried to recruit my Uncle Moses in San Francisco. A brilliant lawyer, he turned the tables on me, asking if I believed in the church because I *wanted* to believe. And did I truly believe? I had to ask myself, could I never recruit anybody because, as a Jew, I never really believed that Rev. Moon or *anyone* could be the Second Coming of Christ?

The seed of doubt planted by my granduncle grew into a forest of distrust when Moon launched a multi-million dollar public relations push supporting President Richard Nixon during the Watergate crisis. When the White House tapes were released, my disbelief reached the breaking point. I fled from the church in the summer of 1974.

Over the next decade, through journal writing and then counseling, I forgave the "Moonies" and myself for what happened. I recognized and accepted that I joined a religious cult because of low self esteem. I then evolved the theory of "authority addiction," and this awareness has helped me reclaim my personal power.

These lessons were reinforced after I entered journalism in 1976. I become a big fish in Denver's small pond as a newspaper columnist and editor. So many new writers came to me for advice that I started a business in 1982 charging for my "wisdom." My arrogance caused the venture to fail by 1984, leaving me deeply in debt.

As an authority addict, my insecurity first drove me to serve a king and later to be a king served by others. I learned how emotional bonds ensnare servants and masters alike, forming a sick symbiosis. Leaders crave followers as followers crave leaders. This dysfunctional loop of *codependent despotism* is evident in any authoritarian regime.

EVERY dictator is an authority addict with childhood boundary issues. We can blame our past for our authority addiction, but it does nothing to alter our current situation. We also can blame despotism on genetic or physical sources, like the disease of George III, but is our biochemistry the *cause* or the *effect* of our personalities?

Recovery from any addiction begins with breaking the old neural patterning behind our addictive behavior. If we overeat, for example, dieting is futile until we can release the unconscious conditioning that equates food with emotions. To replace neural links that harm us with neural links that benefit us, we first need to become conscious of our compulsive habits; then we can change our obsolete behaviors.

Can we change our inherited or learned habits with medicines or deprogramming? Rather than trying a "technological fix" employing pharmaceuticals, genetic therapy or Skinnerian operant conditioning to modify our authoritarian behavior patterns, let's go within and do our personal growth work to get "clean and sober."

Personal growth is our due diligence for democracy. Among our options are 12-Step programs, diverse modes of psychotherapy (such as gestalt, logotherapy, cognitive-emotive therapy, or psychodrama), peer counseling, Reiki, prayer circles, or journaling. Worthy personal growth gurus include Carl Jung, Viktor Frankl, Albert Ellis, Carolyn Myss, and others. Any approach may work, *if* we do the work.

Recovery starts by admitting we are powerless over our addictive urges, which are cunning and baffling. We realize that no other person can remove our shortcomings for us, so we ask for help from God, as we understand God. Instead of controlling others, we ask God to help us control ourselves. Instead of egotistical self will, we seek to know God's will. We experience a spiritual awakening.

As we travel the long road of recovery from authority addiction, our minds and hearts are transformed. We feel serenity or inner peace, which gives us more power to change our behavior. This shift inside is amplified as we start thinking globally. We find a balance between accepting we're powerless to prevent the urges rooted in our past pain and the clear knowledge that our natural global interactivity makes us powerful enough to respond to those urges in a new way.

The journey from darkness into light may take the rest of our lives. We may stumble often, but we keep on keeping on. By accepting total responsibility for the effects of our personalities and our life choices, we can and we will liberate the world by liberating ourselves.

III. Thoughts on the
State of World Affairs

My first wish is to see this plague of mankind,
war, banished from the earth.
          – GEORGE WASHINGTON

11. From Argument to Arms

IN THE following pages I offer nothing more than simple facts, plain arguments, and common sense, and have no other preliminaries to settle with the reader, than that he [or she] will divest himself of prejudice and pre-possession, and suffer his reason and feelings to determine [the truth] for themselves; that he will put on, or rather that he will not put off the true character of a [hu]man, and generously enlarge his [or her] views beyond the present day.

Thomas Paine's thoughts closely parallel my own thinking at this midpoint in the update of his essay.

Volumes have been written on... the struggle between England and America. Men [and women] of all ranks have embarked in the controversy, from different motives, and with various designs; but all have been ineffectual, and the period of debate is closed. Arms, as the last resource, decide the contest; the appeal was the choice of the king, and the continent hath accepted the challenge.

In modern terms, a lot of books have been written from differing viewpoints about the struggle between tyranny and democracy. The time for debate is over. War, as a last resort, is deciding the contest. Today's expanding war was the choice of both the terrorist cults and our government leaders. Our world has accepted the challenge.

Is the war against terrorism worth losing our civil liberties in any country? Must our "homeland defense" laws negate the promises of democracy? Here in the United States, the president has assured us that his draconian security measures are temporary, yet the renewed Patriot Act and related Executive Orders seem as permanent as the secretive Homeland Security Department.

Should a thought so fatal possess us in today's conflict as to let our human rights and liberties be forever canceled for our transient safety, erasing centuries of toil and sacrifice, our names and the names of our ancestors will be despised by future generations.

THE ideal of genuine democracy scares us because it means we have to confront our authority addiction. To create peace in the world, we need peace in our souls. Until our addictive habits feel unbearable enough for us to transform from within, we will persist in pessimism. Why deny the hope of self rule guided by global sense? *Why refuse to give peace a chance when peace is the only chance we've got?*

> The sun never shined on a cause of greater worth. 'Tis not the affair of a city, a country, a province, or a kingdom, but of a continent... [and] the habitable globe. 'Tis not the concern of a day, a year, or an age; [for our] posterity are virtually involved in the contest, and will be more or less affected, even to the end of time, by the proceedings....
>
> Now is the seed time of continental [or global] union, faith and honor. The least fracture now will be like a name engraved with the point of a pin on the tender rind of a young oak; the wound will enlarge with the tree, and posterity [will] read it in full grown characters.
>
> By referring the matter from argument to arms, a new area for politics is struck; a new method of thinking hath arisen. All plans, proposals... prior to the nineteenth of April [1775], i.e., to the commencement of hostilities [the attacks in Massachusetts], are like the almanacs of last year; which, though proper then, are superseded and useless now.

We can say the same thing about our lives since the eleventh of September, 2001, the start of today's hostilities. Our world is not as it was before. Our world will never be as it was before.

Nine months after Lexington and Concord, "the shots heard round the world," Paine faced widespread, entrenched Loyalist sentiments favoring reconciliation with England. Public willingness to demand autonomy and democracy was in grave doubt. Persuading Americans to wage a war for national independence and to form the world's first modern republic was the reason Paine wrote *Common Sense*.

In today's cold climate of insecurity, we're similarly feeling urges favoring reconciliation with our despotic habits—our need for a king. Public willingness to overthrow our inner tyrants and declare spiritual and political unity seems in grave doubt. Persuading us to conduct a social and cultural campaign for personal democracy and world peace is the reason I'm writing *Global Sense.*

Anyone who takes nature as a guide is not easily driven away from the argument that global thinking makes common sense. On the solid ground of logic and my hard-won life lessons, I can propose a general theory: That global sense is a single, simple idea already contained naturally within our true selves, but authority addiction (in the world and in ourselves) is an exceedingly complex, complicated matter that defies nature and natural law. Consider Paine's perspective:

> Whatever was advanced by the advocates on either side of the question then terminated in one and the same point, *viz*, the inevitability of union with Great Britain; the only difference between the parties was the method of effecting it; the one proposing force, the other friendship; but it hath so far happened that the first hath failed, and the second hath withdrawn her influence.

For us today, the social presumption is that strong men astride their thrones will always rule us. Even our women leaders tend to emulate the culturally enshrined male model of authoritarian power. The only question has been whether "alpha males" will take power by force of arms or by force of personality. But the presumption of male rule has now failed. Force and friendship both have betrayed us. The result is an escalating risk of a global catastrophe.

> As much hath been said of the advantages of reconciliation... we should [now] examine the contrary side of the argument, and inquire into some of the... material injuries which these colonies sustain, and always will sustain, by being connected with, and dependent on Great Britain. [We need] to examine that connection and dependence, on the principles of nature and common sense, to see what we have to trust to, if separated [from our reliance upon a king], and what we are to expect, if [we remain] dependent.

Much has been said about the advantages of compliance with the tyrants in our world and within ourselves. But that dream has been shattered by recent events. We awaken to examine the other side of the argument. Let us consider the injuries we suffer, and always will suffer, from our addictive dependence on kings and other masters. Applying the principles of nature and common sense, let us ask, what can we expect if we stay addicted to our abuse of power?

IN THIS chapter, I've alternated between Tom Paine's writing and my updated paraphrasing. Such repetition will soon turn tedious. So, from here on, I will mostly paraphrase him, only quoting Paine where his words fit or his writing soars. If the ideas in any passage are all my own, I'll do my best to make that clear.

Kindly note that I'm mirroring Paine's reasoning but applying it differently. Where he wanted colonists to disavow the king, I want us to disavow all forms of authority addiction. Where he aimed to incite a war for national independence, I aim to inspire a peaceful campaign for global interdependence. We both share a common goal, however, which is advancing the cause of democracy in our times.

Let's review where we've been and where we'll go from here.

In Part I, building upon the Enlightenment thinking that inspired Thomas Paine, I identified the central principles of civil government and mindful self rule, studying how one affects the other.

In Part II, based on Paine's rejection of monarchy and hereditary succession, I explored why we worship authoritarian governments, naming male rule and authority addiction as the root causes.

Here in Part III, where Paine argued against reconciling with the king, I'll argue against enabling authority addiction in the world or in ourselves, explaining why mindful self rule is our best option.

Finally, in Part IV, we'll pull all the pieces together. Where Paine showed how to win a national revolution, I'll suggest ways to win our global evolution. We'll see how each of us can claim the power of our global unity to change the world by changing ourselves.

The people never give up their liberties
but under some delusion.
– EDMUND BURKE

12. Sacrifices to Superstition

PLEASE consider how Tom Paine in 1776 answered arguments in favor of Americans reconciling themselves to the crown.

> I have heard it asserted by some, that as America hath flourished under her former connection with Great Britain, that the same connection is necessary towards her future happiness, and will always have the same effect.

Some today assert the same claim about our connection with some exalted leader being necessary for our future happiness. Paine wrote,

> Nothing can be more fallacious than this kind of argument. We may as well assert, that because a child has thrived upon milk, that it is never to have meat [or vegetables], or that the first twenty years of our lives is to become a precedent for the next twenty.

The truth is that we would have prospered just as much on earth, or more, if we'd never had anything to do with kings. Without kings, we still would have worked hard to enrich ourselves with commerce, perhaps harder, for farmers and grocers will always enjoy a market so long as eating is the custom in our world.

But our kings have protected us, say some. Monarchs and dictators have defended our lives and property at our own expense, as well as their own at times; that's true. But such public defense stems from the same motive as those in business, for the sake of market domination. The tyrants were defending themselves, not us.

> Alas! we have been long led away by ancient prejudices and made large sacrifices to superstition.

We've boasted of protection by kings and their minions, but we have rarely considered that their motive always was self interest, not world service. Do not be fooled by clever speechwriters.

Despotic leaders do not protect us from enemies for our benefit. They protect themselves from the enemies they created on their own, and we hide under their shield. Their foes have no real quarrel with us except for our choice of leadership. They will remain our enemies while we keep those leaders. Most Middle-Eastern people do not hate the American people, for instance, so much as the policies and actions of the U.S. Government, which are not above reproach.

Let all the kings wave their lies before the world like flags. Now is the time for humanity to throw off reliance on them, so we can live in peace. The misery of war ought to warn us against trusting any tyrant, whether in government or in our unconscious minds.

ANOTHER claim is that we can have no real relationship to each other but through some heroic leader. Logically, this is a fallacy.

Let's identify our true connection. Our 21st century science agrees the whole of life is interacting at the subtlest levels in our universe. Literally, *all life is light,* or energy slowed down into matter, vibrating below the threshold of $E=MC^2$. Additionally, all of the atoms in our bodies were birthed in exploding stars. We are stardust. As the Lakota say, *hau mitakuye oyas'in* (all my relations). All life is one.

But instead of unity in enlightenment, we consent to a false unity. We let leaders demonize a common enemy as the "Great Satan" who threatens us. Binding us under their leadership, this ruse is the oldest trick in the book, and it still works, as recent events prove.

This sly strategy was articulated by U.S. journalist H.L. Mencken, "The whole aim of practical politics is to keep the populace alarmed and hence, clamorous to be led to safety—by menacing it with an endless series of hobgoblin, all of them imaginary."

Beware when the enemies of our masters become our enemies. Our only kinship with one another then is suffering and death. Wrote Voltaire, "Those who can make you believe absurdities can make you commit atrocities."

DOES birth or adoption in a mother country unites us? If we admit the United States mistreated its adopted children—Native Americans and immigrants alike—then Americans can't deny our connection in shame. Nor can we deny our tacit consent to CIA assassinations and coups around the world (as the CIA did in Chile on Sept. 11, 1973), or the recent torture of war prisoners by U.S. troops and by surrogates after kidnapping and "rendition" to secret prisons in Eastern Europe. If humanity is one family, we're a deeply dysfunctional family.

Despite moral failures, the American and European democracies have become the hope and asylum for the tormented lovers of liberty escaping every tyranny around the planet. These refugees did not flee the tender embrace of a mother. They fled the cruelty of a monster. The very same ancient habits of despotism that first drove frightened emigrants from their homes still pursue their descendants.

Are we united by having a *fatherland, motherland* or *homeland* in common? That cultural "construct" happens not to be true.

Even if all life on earth sprang from primordial ooze, the ground itself does not gives birth to humans now. We may feel affinity for the land or soil, but love binds us to the earth, not deeds or titles. Let's stand on the ground of provable facts and clear thinking. Defending territory is merely animal instinct, like a dog marking turf.

Historically, kings and dictators have used the emotionally loaded terms of *fatherland, motherland* and *homeland* to control the gullible, unthinking masses. Our natural needs for "home, family and security" have been manipulated at our expense. Why must we sacrifice our hearts, minds and blood for any nation with man-made borders when the full compass of the globe is our abode?

In the extensive parts of the world map called the United States of America, for example, we may forget the limits of 3.6 million square miles of territory. Instead, many of us in this land of my birth feel our friendships on a global scale. We triumph in the generosity of the feeling. The same may be said of the inhabitants in every land today who are "thinking globally and acting locally."

> It is pleasant to observe by what regular gradations we surmount the force of local prejudice, as we enlarge our acquaintance with the world. [A man born in any town who meets a neighbor many miles from home] drops the narrow idea of a street, and salutes him by the name of townsman.... And by a just parity of reasoning, Europeans meeting in America, or any other quarter of the globe, are countrymen; [they are not bound by national] distinctions too limited for continental [or global] minds.

Before Paine wrote *Common Sense*, people thought of each colony in the Americas as a separate country. He persuaded colonists from New York to Georgia to see themselves as part of one new nation. Just as Europe's nations today seek to form a European Union, people in all lands now need to see themselves as part of one world. Instead of "homeland" meaning one country only, we need to see that usage as false, selfish and narrow, for the whole earth truly is our home.

PAINE now turned his attention to convincing American colonists that reconciling with the crown would be pure folly. His remarks also fit reconciling ourselves to authority addiction.

> Though I would carefully avoid giving unnecessary offense, yet I am inclined to believe, that all those who espouse the doctrine of reconciliation [with regal power], may be included within the following descriptions:

Paine named self-interested people who cannot be trusted, weak or prejudiced people who cannot see the truth, and moderate people who think better of the world than it deserves. This last class contains most of the population. Too few of us ever take time to consider the nature of life, our own inner nature or the way we affect the world. *The great mass of unthinking people in every land may be the tragic source of more calamities on our planet than all other causes combined.*

Many of us on earth share the good fortune of living distant from the scenes of sorrow elsewhere around the globe. The evils of despair, ignorance and poverty are too rarely brought home to our doors in the "developed" parts of the world. We rarely feel the fragility of our own lives in an interactive world of suffering. We see to our own comforts only. We suspect the needy are faking their anguish.

For compassion, let your imagination carry you inside the World Trade Center on September 11, 2001. Join the police officers and fire fighters as they race up the stairwells; imagine what they hear as the floors above plunge down onto them. Now see yourself on one of the disaster crews pulling body parts from the gruesome debris.

Next, put yourself in the place of Afghani women under the burkha after the 9/11 attacks. Long repressed by the Taliban men measuring holiness (testosterone) by the length of their beards, you look up to see U.S. warplanes overhead dropping bombs. Freedom from male rule is offset by fear of losing your children. Now put yourself in the besieged nation of Iraq as U.S.-led troops cross the border; you want the dictator deposed, yet you dread colonial occupation.

Finally, let yourself feel the anguish of those dying from hunger or disease in Africa, Asia, or Latin America. See life through the eyes of the billion people on the globe without clean drinking water. Stand in the shoes of the 40 million Americans facing poverty without hope.

If we can feel true compassion for anyone on earth, how can we accept suffering anywhere on earth?

TOM Paine addressed the Americans who wanted to overlook the rights abuses by the British monarchy, who wanted all the colonies to stay under the crown. People of passive tempers today may likewise wish to lightly overlook all the problems from authoritarian thinking in our world. Such foolish people are

> still hoping for the best, are apt to call out, 'Come we shall be friends again for all this.' But examine the passions and feelings of [hu]mankind. Bring the doctrine of reconciliation to the touch-stone of nature, and then tell me, whether you can hereafter love, honor, and faithfully serve the power that hath carried fire and sword into your land?... [If you] can still shake hands with the murderers, then... whatever may be your rank or title in life, you have the heart of a coward, and the spirit of a sycophant.

Paine's goal with these harsh words was to motivate people to grab their guns or empty their purses to support the rebellion. My goal here is to motivate nonviolent activism. Yet in Paine's spirit, I must ask, are we likewise ignoring crimes by our government? Along with the points raised in Chapter 5, for example, look at how the President sent troops to fight an unjustified war without enough armor to stay alive. He then cut their pay, cut the health benefits for veterans who survive, and cut the death benefits for the families of those killed.

> I mean not to exhibit horror for the [bitter] purpose of provoking revenge, but to awaken us from [our] fatal and unmanly [or inhumane] slumbers, that we may pursue determinately some fixed object.

It is not in the power of any despot to conquer the spirit of those willing to be true to themselves with a clear mind and the heart of a peaceful warrior. Armies cannot conquer ideas. *The present winter of our discontent is worth an age if rightly employed for positive action.* Our worldly honors do not matter. There is no reproach we will not deserve from posterity for any failure to act in this global crisis that sacrifices today's precious and useful season.

PAINE invited his reader to move beyond their fear of freedom.

> I have heard some men say, many of whom I believe spoke without thinking, that they dreaded independence, fearing it would produce civil wars.

Seldom are such reactionary thoughts correct, he wrote. We have more reasons to dread the security of dependence than the insecurity of independence, or the duties of interdependence, I'd add.

We common people have shown a natural spirit of good order and cooperation with constitutional governments. Our historic example ought to suffice for any reasonable person to feel confident that we *are* capable of responsible self rule. Given deep literacy and access to the information we need to think for ourselves, no one can assign the least credence to fears of us destroying ourselves if empowered to vote directly on the public policies governing our lives.

In any land where democratic values govern individuals, markets and governments, that land is prone to liberty and peace. Any political party upholding these principles will win public favor. *If libertarians and progressives unite to advocate personal and social responsibility balanced by calls for smaller government and less state intrusion into private lives, the coalition could win most elections.*

I believe humanity is capable of real democracy, but we're being stopped cold by old fears of misusing our freedom. I believe humanity is ready to mature beyond war, but we dread responsible adulthood. We are like the fallen toddler afraid to rise and keep on walking.

For years I've clung to the false belief from my childhood that I'm not good enough to have what I want in life, that I'm my own worst enemy, that I'll always fail. I've kept this programming hidden from my consciousness. Since what we hide from our awake minds forms our shadow selves, I've been ruled by my shadow.

Only with decades of counseling and personal growth workshops have I dared to trust myself enough to dive into the ocean of sadness inside and cry out my tears of grief. Only by naming my fears have I gained power over them. Only by facing and forgiving the pain within have I found the joy to go after my dreams, such as writing this book. Unless I risk failure, how can I hope to succeed?

How many of us permit our fears to block us from self realization, from maturing into the responsibility and integrity of global thinking? This principle for individuals applies equally to society.

Good government asks the people to solve problems and disputes based on fact and reason. In conflicts like those between Israelis and Palestinians, or between Muslims and Hindus, we need to halt raw brutality without becoming brutes ourselves. We need to learn how to disagree without becoming disagreeable.

THE utmost stretch of our wisdom cannot offer any plan short of separation from our authority addiction that promises the world even one day of certain peace. Enabling power addicts in hopes of security always was and will be an absurd fantasy and fatal fallacy.

Every quiet strategy for social liberation has been ineffectual. The nonviolent protests of Mahatma Gandhi and Martin Luther King were never quiet. If our prayers for peace seemed rejected by God, it's only because we've refused to accept personal and social responsibility for co-creating the world with our God. As President John F. Kennedy said, "Here on earth, God's work must truly be our own."

> For God's sake, let us come to a final separation, and not
> leave the next generation to be cutting throats, under the
> ...unmeaning names of parent and child [or homeland].

It would be foolish to say that once every terrorist and dictator is jailed or killed, despots will never again try to force themselves on the world. Weapons of mass destruction still abound around our world, from biological and electronic bugs to nuclear bombs. Can we ever be safe from terror while the "war on terrorism" drags on?

Look at how anti-war demonstrators calling for peace are being investigated by security agencies like the FBI, the same as during the Vietnam war era. Witness how demonstrators at political conventions are confined in "free speech zones." (Seems to me that everywhere on earth should be a free speech zone.) Recall the unprecedented army of black-clad police gathered from across the nation in Washington, DC, for the second inauguration of President George W. Bush.

If our leaders in the United States, or in any nation, are unwilling to hear our dissent, how can we trust their leadership? We must grow alarmed when they act like Soviet dictator Joseph Stalin, who said, "Ideas are far more powerful than guns. We don't allow our enemies to have guns. Why should we allow them to have ideas?"

Through books like this one, and through all related instruments of mass instruction, we may deduce that if we fail to renounce war and political repression now, we may never get another chance like today to insist on the moral accountability of our governments.

In the same way, we may never get another chance like today to insist on the moral accountability of our own selves. As I've begun opening my mind to global thinking, as I've begun to see how my life choices affect the planet, I've changed my daily habits, from where I shop to what I eat to how I vote.

My growth process is slow, yet I have steadily matured. While I do not yet embody my ideals, while I'm still quite flawed, I am thinking globally as best I can. I have seen how changing my thoughts changes my life. Surely I'm not exceptional in this regard. If you look at the effects of global thinking in your own life, I bet you can see changes for the better, too. What improvements can you name?

As a deep sense of our global oneness spreads throughout society, as more of us cultivate global mindfulness, the opportunity to do our personal growth work has never been greater, nor has the need. Now we know the truth: Our own redemption redeems the world.

If we allow hope for democracy and world peace to be defeated in our minds during this formative period, the chance for success will pass us by. Would we ever again have the heart to revive our debate about the pitiless ideology of the New World Order? Could we ever again mount a global campaign for self liberation?

It is to be feared when America has
consolidated its despotism, the world
will witness the truth of the assertion.
— MERCY OTIS WARREN

13. The Tyrants' Last Stand

MUCH has been said about the united strength of society under dictators. Fielding vast armies like Alexander, Julius Caesar, Genghis Khan, Napoleon, Hitler, Stalin, or Mao, we may defeat all others to rule the world. We can defy all while chanting, "Might makes right."

But this is mere presumption; the fate of war is uncertain, neither do the expressions mean anything.

People in our world today will never willingly suffer the entire planet to be drained of all inhabitants to support any leader's arrogant pride. When our survival is at stake, we *will* act to save ourselves.

Besides, what have we to do with setting the world at defiance? Our plan is commerce, and that, well attended to, will secure [for] us the peace and friendship [of the world].

Ample prosperity from free and fair trade is our best guard against conquest by any master, from within or from without. It's in the best interest of the world, therefore, to have every nation as an open port. Healthy grain will fetch its due price in any open market on earth, for quality products will be bought by those left free to prosper. We'd need no master *if* we'd let Adam Smith's invisible hand (guided by sympathy) liberate markets from monopolies, *if* we'd create world trade bodies accountable to citizens not corporations.

I challenge those advocating compliance with regal power (in any disguise) to prove one lasting advantage that we or the world can reap by continuing to serve authoritarian masters.

I repeat the challenge, not a single advantage is derived.

The injuries and disadvantages we suffer from our ties to haughty male rule at all levels of society are beyond counting. Our moral duty to humanity and ourselves is to reject any alliance with tyranny.

Further, our compliance with competitive despots tends to involve us in fierce quarrels and wars, which sets us at odds with other people,

> who would otherwise seek our friendship, and against whom, we have neither anger nor complaint.

Our world is too thickly planted with tyrants to stay long at peace. Whenever a war breaks out because of them, local and world trade goes to ruin, such as we see happening today.

Individuals and nations alike are wise to steer clear of the disputes of kings and would-be kings. But we can never do this so long as we stay emotionally dependent on our leaders for personal and national security, so long as we refuse to practice mindful self rule.

If we feel too captivated by our fears to choose freedom, we let our authority addiction tip the scales of politics and society. We invite the sort of thinking that Orwell and Huxley clearly warned us against in *Nineteen Eighty-Four* and *Brave New World*.

> Every thing that is right or natural pleads for [a speedy] separation [from a dependence on kings]. The blood of the slain, the weeping voice of nature cries, 'tis time to part.

Please consider how the natural law of our global interdependence connects each one of us on earth equally. Seems to me this is a strong and rational proof that absolute authority of one person over another was never included in the intelligent design of the cosmos. Tyranny descends only from the darkest human designs, never from God.

REFLECT on the idea of leaders trying to conquer the world.

Logically, it's not in the power of any centralized authority to do the world justice. How can a global power so distant from us, thus so ignorant of us, manage our lives with any tolerable degree of ability? If aloof leaders cannot understand us, how can they govern us?

As the people governed under any global empire, our lives would be miserable. We'd always be running halfway around the world with our petitions and explanations. Any reply we received would require teams of experts to explain it to us. The muddle would be worse than with any national government. Such a global system, as Paine wrote,

> will in a few [short] years be looked upon as folly and childishness.

Paine pointed out the absurdity of one small island ruling a great continent an ocean away. It's equally absurd for America or for any one nation to rule the world, which is the fantasy of every dictator. Why should we forever strive to dominate others like bullies?

Pockets of poverty incapable of feeding or protecting themselves may be proper objects of remote governance, which must end as the people learn self sufficiency. But it's inane to believe free adults must be governed perpetually as children.

In no instance has nature made the offspring of a species forever dependent on the parents after birth. For humanity to stay forever as children reverses the order of nature, violating natural law. Rationally, the design of creation is that we're each meant to mature into aware adults able to handle free will responsibly. To persist in believing we must forever stay as children is, in itself, childish and ridiculous.

The attitude in the world toward paternalism is like a youth who is ready to be done with dependence on the parents, who cares little about the insecurity of liberty. Like that youth, we want the freedom to learn from our mistakes, for how else can we grow?

Any government that fails to protect the power of common people to become mature adults is unworthy of its power. Such a grim regime is no government at all. It lacks moral legitimacy by any enlightened standard, so the people pay their taxes for nothing.

KINGS have always negated our independence, you may say, for common people have never enacted laws without a king's consent. A telling point of right and good order. Tyrants in all ages have proven themselves to be the staid enemy of democracy.

But there's something odd in the idea of any king like George III saying to several million people, "There shall be no laws but such as I like." This fits any son of a George presuming to be much wiser than the millions of us who question his right to rule over us.

If we forget about democracy and accept despotism as inevitable, the result would be the ruin of our world. Government would stay in the grasping hands of authority addicts who will work to prevent all legislation that helps us learn to practice personal democracy.

Power addicts will never gladly permit the passage of any law that takes away the unnatural powers that people granted to them in hasty fear. Is there anyone so unwise as not to realize (given recent events) that the puppet masters now in control will suffer no laws to be made that do not suit their purpose of always pulling the strings? Can you doubt their goal is to manipulate our hearts and minds?

The constitutions in most democracies let legislatures make almost no laws without a president enacting the bill with a signature. Rarely is a presidential veto overridden. In the United States, for example, how many worthy measures perish in House or Senate subcommittees after a hallway murmur the White House may veto a proposal? This situation surely is mirrored in other nations.

Of course, cynical leaders will scarcely oppose to any law giving them more authority over us, such as the Patriot Acts. Yet we may be as effectively enslaved by the lack of laws protecting our rights as by the passage of laws unduly reducing our liberties. The point is that too many leaders make laws to serve their own interests, not ours.

Very few rulers are qualified by training or instinct for leadership roles. By needing to be needed, they make more promises than they can keep. Those tend to exhibit a sort of Munchausen Syndrome by Proxy—secretly hurting those in their care, then rushing to the rescue to claim heroic glory. Anyone pointing out their crime is called a liar. *So, if a craving to rule the world is proof of insanity, all would-be kings and messiahs are inherently unfit for leadership.*

Popular disdain for most leaders today reflects our suspicion that anybody who seeks public office cannot be trusted with power. The broadbrush smear of "politician" scares off many worthy people from entering public service. And here is another way that despots damage us: Their misconduct keeps good people out of government.

WE COULD never stop exposing the wild absurdities of authority addiction, but what answer best suits our world today?

Look at any nation on earth where leaders rule and the common people do not. The people asserting their rights face more danger than the leaders refusing to admit the people have any rights at all.

What if public opinion demanded a repeal of all the new insecurity laws? If leaders felt they could stay in power one day longer by co-opting the popular will, they would revoke the laws today, providing we left them in office. They'd do by fraud in the long run what they cannot do by fear in the short run, for their ends justify their means. Because of such ruthless cunning by authority addicts, Paine wrote,

"Reconciliation and ruin are nearly related."

Kings and other masters will cling to power as long as we let them. Any deals we make to appease them postpones real self government, delaying the maturation of our species. The general state of the world, meanwhile, will be like life for the 13 afflicted American colonies if they'd struck a deal with the crown short of full national sovereignty. Such a future of unhealthy codependency would be forever tottering on the brink of commotion and disturbance.

The denial of our natural rights already spawns dissent. The effects of violence, such as rioting by anti-war protesters or by repressed races and classes, may be more deadly to the planet than the merged malice of every king or dictator. The danger is real.

Nothing short of ending authority addiction will help us now. As a viable alternative to male rule, we need to learn how mindful self rule guided by global sense empowers us, like Thoreau, to live deliberately and peacefully. What else can reasonably prevent future wars?

IS IMAGINING humanity free from tyranny a useless waste? For the Americans afraid of separation from British rule, Paine wrote,

> I am not induced by [the] motives of pride, party, or resentment to espouse the doctrine of separation and independence... Every thing short of that [separation] is mere patchwork, that it can afford no lasting felicity, that it is leaving the sword to our children, and shrinking back at a time, when, a little more, a little farther, would have rendered this continent the glory of the earth.

His words apply on a global scale. The cultural force of male rule in society hasn't shown the least interest in compromise. All the kings on earth would control every aspect of our lives if we let them.

Consider the costs in blood and treasure we've already paid for freedom from kings. Count the losses in lives and property. No terms of reconciliation with our inherited authority addiction can ever be negotiated that would leave us safe from destruction.

Those of us lacking global sense may not feel we've ever suffered at the hands of dictators. The petty boss at work or in a community group may not bother us, especially if our daily lives are comfortable, so we tolerate their abuses. But what if all we possess is at risk? What if our home may be bulldozed or if those we love may be killed if we assert our rights? Will we still stand up for freedom?

The core dispute is for control over our bodies, minds, hearts, and souls. The value of a pursued object must bear a fair ratio to the cost of gaining it. Therefore, most leaders waste their time and resources trying to manage the unmanageable. The only person on earth who has the right and talent to rule your life is *you*. You alone possess the power of consent, which is the power for mindful self rule.

What if we desire to change or repeal laws enacted without our comment or consent? What if we oppose policies suspending our civil liberties in the name of our safety? What if we want leaders to accept accountability for their power abuses? Dare we protest?

I would *not* foment a revolt as Paine did in 1776. For democracy with freedom and justice for all, instead of becoming violent citizen soldiers, we now need to become peaceful citizen activists.

We have many examples of courage to inspire us.

In the last century, recall the nonviolent civil rights movement in America and a grassroots movement to end the U.S. war in Vietnam. Recall the nonviolent mass demonstration for democracy in China's Tienanmen Square, how one man alone stood up to a Red Army tank. Recall the mostly peaceful revolutions in Eastern Europe when the Berlin Wall fell and the people toppled the Soviet empire.

Already in the 21st century, recall record-breaking protests against the U.S.-led invasion of Iraq. Recall Venezuelans arising to thwart a U.S.-backed coup against their elected president. Recall Ukrainians fighting vote fraud by occupying Kiev's Square of Independence until winning a new runoff election. Recall peaceful protests in Ecuador, coordinated by la Luna Radio, that capsized a corrupt government. Recall a million youth in Paris streets reversing an unjust job law. Recall millions protesting in Nepal until the king restored parliament. Recall any time where the people fought city hall and won.

Such successes amply prove the impact of people power.

I'VE long seen world peace as an evolutionary event that sooner or later must arrive. Given today's global awakening, world peace need not be far off. Must more generations suffer by our delay?

> No [person] was a warmer wisher for reconciliation
> than myself, before the fatal nineteenth of April, 1775
> (Massacre at Lexington), but the moment the event of
> that day was made known, I rejected the hardened, sullen
> tempered Pharaoh of England for ever.

We can say the same about the fatal eleventh of September, 2001. Since that day, many of us reject forever our addiction to authority. We renounce the insanity of war, empire and world conquest.

"Naturally the common people don't want war," said Nazi leader Hermann Göring. "But after all, it is the leaders of the country who determine policy, and it is always a simple matter to drag the people along.... All you have to do is to tell them they are being attacked, and denounce the pacifists for [their] lack of patriotism and exposing the country to danger. It works the same in any country."

If it's true that nationalism can cloak itself as patriotism to fool the people, a question arises: How can any leader claiming to represent us unfeelingly drag us into war and then revoke our civil rights on the grounds they do not trust us to act responsibly?

Do our leaders know us? Do they know whether we've evolved a global sense of unity with all life that renders violence unthinkable? No, they do not know us, but they presume to decide for us. Their faith lay in Theory X and the cynicism of Hobbes. We are presumed guilty of original sin, collective guilt or widespread stupidity. Thus, our leaders fail to give us any vote before revoking our right to vote. *Our governments rule in our name but without our consent.*

How can elected leaders in the United States or in any land sleep well tonight with such a grave betrayal of democracy on their souls? Indeed, how can any of us on earth enjoy untroubled sleep now, while freedom itself endures in peril?

Thomas Jefferson declared, "I have sworn upon the altar of God eternal hostility against every form of tyranny over the mind of man." Will we join him to free our minds from authority addiction?

We thought we'd fought a war to end all wars in World War I. We thought we'd made the world safe for democracy in World War II. We thought world peace was at hand when the Soviet empire fell, ending the cold war. But the rise of new horrors in places like the Balkans, Middle East, Sudan, and Indonesia soon disillusioned us.

Millions throughout human history have been injured or murdered by arrogant barbarity. Will billions more now suffer this tragic fate? In Afghanistan, Iraq, and next perhaps Iran or Syria, are we seeing the first rounds of U.S. military actions that could escalate into our global annihilation? Brothers in the "promised land" fighting over the legacy of Abraham threaten us all, for suicide bombings by Palestinians hurt chances for peace as much as the West Bank and Gaza Strip apartheid barriers built by Israel. The cycle of hate and war must end.

An elite fraction of us controls most of the wealth on earth. Instead of enjoying God's abundance, a fear of scarcity has distorted property laws under both capitalism and socialism. Both economic systems are compatible with democracy, but neither system today is genuinely democratic. Both systems at their extremes breed dictatorships.

Unless we change our worldview, unless we change our personal relationship with power, logic tells us, much of humanity could perish from wars, plagues, or environmental disasters.

We stand at the crossroads. Will we abide more tedious tyrannies, or will we construct creative democracies? Will we descend into stark oppression more terrifying than the darkest cyberpunk nightmares, or will we ascend toward an enlightened civilization? Shall we destroy ourselves, or will we fulfill our highest aspirations?

Humanity at last is outgrowing a need for competitive male rule. The pendulum is swinging back toward feminine cooperation. We're aiming for a balance promoting peace and liberty. Thus, our despotic past desperately seeks to regain its stranglehold over us.

In the lust for empire by the United States, Russia, China, or other countries, in the drive for world market domination by multinational corporations, in the struggle by extremist Christians and Muslims and messianic cults to impose a theocracy, in the push by white men to assert power over women and other races, we are seeing the tyrants' last stand. Enough is enough.

If we release our authority addiction now, we may be free at last.

Were there a people of gods, their
government would be democratic.
— JEAN JACQUES ROUSSEAU

14. A Government of Our Own

DESPOTISM and democracy have different owners. Despotism belongs to the tyrant alone. Democracy belongs to us all.

> A government of our own is our natural right. And when a man seriously reflects on the precariousness of human affairs, he will become convinced, that... [if we fail to create a government of our own] some Massenello* may hereafter arise, who laying hold of popular disquietudes, may collect together the desperate and the discontented, and by assuming to themselves the powers of government, may sweep away the liberties of the continent like a deluge.

Thomas Paine knew that without intelligent self rule, our ancient chaotic habits of self loathing and self destruction will continue, and

> the tottering situation [meanwhile]... will be a temptation for some desperate adventurer to try his fortune.

Society is full of would-be messiahs awaiting their chance to save the world in trade for the political power to rule our lives for us. In our interconnected age, if a tyrant rises to power in any nation, before news of the unhappy business can reach our media screens, we may already suffer a loss of our liberty. Paine knew this intuitively.

> Under our present [condition as] British subjects we can neither be received nor heard abroad. The custom of all courts is against us, and will be, until, by independence, we take rank with other nations.

In our present condition as authority addicts, we cannot stand as free individuals in the world, nor can our calls for liberty be heard. All the authoritarian customs of history are against self liberation and real

---

* Called *Massenello*, fisherman Thomas Anello in 1647 stirred up the people in the Naples marketplace against Spanish military occupation. Paine wrote in his footnote that Massenello "prompted them to revolt, and in the space of a day became king."

democracy. Until we do our personal growth work for self rule, until we free our own minds from the legacy of alpha male rule, we'll stay stuck in the immaturity that enables dictators to rule us.

Humanity will evolve from our representative republics into direct republics and genuine democracies only when we adapt to our global interactivity. Public advocacy for global thinking helps us to become accountable adults. Evolving the global sense to live free responsibly is crucial for human survival. Such an awakening is our best hope for civil liberty and lasting peace on earth.

Driven by necessity, we *will* make the shift into global thinking and thus begin practicing mindful self rule and personal democracy. *Global sense is necessary and sufficient for peace and democracy.* Sustain faith in our ultimate success. Trust what Washington wrote: "Liberty, when it begins to take root, is a plant of rapid growth."

> **MANY** strong and striking reasons may be given, to show that nothing can settle our affairs so expeditiously as an open and determined declaration for independence.

Paine's words were prophetic. Six months later, when Americans published the Declaration of Independence, history changed. Must we now publish a declaration of our global interdependence? Could this help shift our world into wholistic thinking? Perhaps, but a far more effective act would be an inner declaration of self liberation.

In my life, I've migrated from codependency toward autonomy by facing my childhood fears and cultivating global sense. My repressed love-hate feelings toward my father drove me to serve a father figure in a cult, then to become an arrogant local celebrity. When I see how my shadow self overrode my true self, how can I not weep? I've since chosen to live with more authenticity. What about you?

As an experiment, list how you've suffered from all the tyrants in yourself, like the way a need for instant gratification makes you act without thinking. Next, list the ways you've denied your part in any problem, like blaming those you've hurt through rash impulsiveness. Reflect on these lists until you can see that you'll never live happily or safely while authoritarian thoughts control your life, that you need mindful self rule. Declaring a commitment to recovery from addictive habits will do the world more good than any act of rebellion.

Ye that oppose independence [or interdependence] now,
ye know not what ye do; ye are opening a door to eternal
tyranny, by keeping vacant the seat of [self] government.

If we expel from our hearts and minds that barbarous and hellish
power that can stir up our inner demons to destroy us, would we think
it glorious? Tyrants let us escape from the obligations of free will by
killing our faith in our own reason, conscience and spirit. To speak of
friendship with any merciless fiend is lunacy.

Why wait even one more day to throw off the ancient yoke of blind
servitude burdening our souls? Paine saw it was too late to reconcile
America and Britain in 1776. And in our global age today, it's too late
to reconcile our souls to authority addiction.

Monitor newscasts to see the consequences of despotic thinking.
Look at the blatant racism against the survivors of Hurricane Katrina.
Look at the looming civil war between Sunnis and Shiites in Iraq. The
harm is undeniable. Given the magnitude of mass deaths lately, our
chronic dogmatic habits have reached the breaking point. The looping
illogic from split perceptions have made the case for self liberation.
We must heal our hidden wounds before we destroy ourselves.

We are like sleepers suddenly roused from listless slumber by cold
water dumped on our beds. We may not welcome our awakening, but
now that our eyes are opened to the power of our global interactivity,
we cannot go back to thinking and living in a stupor as we did before.
We must accept accountability for the effects of our choices.

Wanting us to stay asleep, despots at every level of society work
hard to obstruct democracy and peace. From the boss in the factory or
office to the autocrats leading our governments, they inflict injuries
against body and soul that violate the justice of natural law.

> **COMMON** sense will tell us, that the power which hath
> endeavored to subdue us, is of all others the most improper
> to defend us. Conquest may be effected under the pretense
> of friendship; and ourselves, after a long and brave
> resistance, be at last cheated into slavery.

To update Thomas Paine, common sense says that a power trying
to hurt us cannot be trusted to save us. Our authority addiction may
lure us with promises of security, but our habits betray us into slavery.

In today's crisis, we cannot afford to wait for salvation by a messiah. If we must save ourselves, why not do it for our highest good? If we want peace, we need to break the cycle of hate and violence. Dr. Phil McGraw says, "Stand up and walk out of your history."

Some assert that there must be justice before there can be peace. If by "justice" we mean restitution, repentance and forgiveness on all sides, I'd agree. Peace emerges from justice as justice emerges from peace. But if by "justice" we mean revenge, let's release our grudges. An eye for an eye and a tooth for a tooth leaves us blind and toothless. Refusing to forgive other people locks us into our resentments, which only hurts us, not those whom we resent. Forgiveness frees us from our past pain, so we can feel peace and move on.

Tyrannical acts by the English king sparked a violent revolution in Tom Paine's times, but today we need peaceful evolution. Thoreau in *Civil Disobedience* told how nonviolence overcomes state repression by winning hearts and minds in the court of public opinion.

Yet even as we pledge nonviolence in our pursuit of social justice, the precedent of doing our personal growth work and recovering from authority addiction explicitly threatens those still compelled by their insecurities to rule others. They would stifle our protests, so their own sleep is not disturbed by our appeals to conscience.

Many people claim violence is justified if our lives are threatened. Take the 1943 case of the Jews trapped in Warsaw's ghetto. Boarding trains to Nazi concentration camps or else firing rifles from rooftops meant death for them either way, so why not fight back? That's a trick question. If a spiteful 1918 treaty ending World War I had not blocked Germany's economic recovery, resentful German voters would never have elected Hitler in 1932, so Nazis would not have invaded Poland. Warsaw's Jews would not have faced a choice to kill or be killed.

Martin Luther King advised us, "Nonviolence means avoiding not only external physical violence but also internal violence of the spirit. You not only refuse to shoot a man, but you refuse to hate him." What dissolves anger and even hatred is empathy. If you feel angry at me, yet I treat you with loving respect, can you stay angry?

We have a right to feel angry about the power abuses in our world. Anger can be energizing, but when it drives revenge, we forget about the compassion that invites honest healing. As Ben Franklin warned, "Whatever is begun in anger ends in shame."

One of my hardest life lessons has been that below my anger lurks fear. If I'm angry at anybody, in almost every instance, I'm projecting some aspect of my own shadow onto that person. My flash of anger at another's selfishness may hide a fear of seeing my own selfishness. It's easier to make others wrong than to accept responsibility for my own faults. It's easier to see the mote in your eye than in mine.

Granted, if a person violates a boundary I've plainly declared and defended, like when I ask a co-worker not to eat the food I brought for lunch but that person eats the food anyway, my anger is merited. But in most cases, my anger at others really is anger at myself.

When I harbor a resentment at some old injury, the real issue is my refusal to practice forgiveness. I first need to forgive myself, and then I can forgive others. I need to remind myself that we all do the best we can—given what we know at the time. If I am forever ripping the scab off an old wound, it can never heal. I need to let it be. Once I stop trying to change the past, once I accept what's happened, I can let go of my anger. I can acknowledge my sorrow and grieve my loss. This process invariably opens my heart to compassion.

No matter how much we feel angry or afraid, in this moment now, we can own our pain and find peace. We can listen to our inner voice of reason telling us that hate and violence never make us feel better. We can accept conflict as natural in life, accept our global oneness, let go of shame or blame, and welcome the joy of forgiveness.

A global sensibility helps us heal our resentments by connecting us to the suffering of others. When suicide bombers spark your rage, can you instead feel sadness for all the hate still in our world? *Cultivating compassion, we reap the fruits of love. Sowing forgiveness, we harvest the miracle of peace.* This holds true for individuals and nations.

> The Almighty hath implanted [with]in us these inextinguishable feelings for good and wise purposes. They are the guardians of His [or Her or Its] image in our hearts. They distinguish us from the herd of common animals.
>
> The social compact would dissolve, and justice be extirpated [from] the earth, or have only a casual existence, were we callous to the touches of affection. The robber and the murderer would escape unpunished, did not the injuries which our tempers sustain, provoke us into justice.

> Ye that love [hu]mankind! Ye that dare oppose, not only
> the tyranny, but the tyrant, stand forth! Every spot of the old
> world is overrun with oppression. Freedom hath been
> hunted round the globe.

Every continent on earth has expelled genuine democracy. Some
nations settle for indirect republics—weighted to favor the privileged
classes—yet dictators and monarchs still abound, and even emperors.
Most countries distrust real freedom. Mindful self rule and personal
democracy are dreaded like a stranger coming unbidden to the door.
We howl desperate alarms for liberty to depart. Let's instead join with
Thomas Paine in his eternal call of welcome to democracy:

> O! receive the fugitive, and prepare in time an asylum
> for [hu]mankind.

IV.Our Ability for Democracy and World Peace

There are times when the greatest change
needed is a change of my viewpoint.
— DENIS DIDEROT

15. Common Global Sense

NOW we arrive at the most important question in our discussion. How do we turn global ideals into local realities? Is this possible?

I have never met with a man... in England or America, who hath not confessed his opinion, that a [final] separation between the countries would take place one time or other.

Updating Tom Paine's words, I have rarely met anyone in the U.S. or any other country who, if asked, has not voiced a belief that world peace would emerge someday, even if in the distant future.

And there is no instance in which we have shown less judgment, than in endeavoring to describe what we call, the ripeness or fitness of the Continent for independence.

What about our fitness for global interdependence? Are we ready to develop an open global network of national democracies? Are we ready to accept our individual responsibility for sustaining a balance between self interest and public interest? Are we ready for humanity to leave alpha male rule behind? As we enter the age of globalization, are we ready for a world social contract rooted in global sense?

Humanity now must adapt to the fact of our global connectivity, or else we could perish from the earth. The crux is whether we define "globalization" as the establishment of a corporate superstate above all nations, or if we instead define the term as a process of awakening to an enlightened sense of our global unity in diversity.

Indicating our cultural readiness, a color photograph of our planet is gradually transforming our attitudes. When we look at this famous image, taken by an Apollo XVII astronaut on America's last manned trip to the moon in 1972, we see no lines between nations. We can't pretend any longer to be living apart from one another. We can't think of our lives as we did before this icon penetrated our hearts.

In the photograph, we can sense the connection between world events and our part in creating these events. We realize that we are "co-creators." Each one of us holds personal and social responsibility for the global consequences of our private and public choices. We can see that the creative power to change the world truly rests with "we the people." Seeing our global interactivity, we know that improving 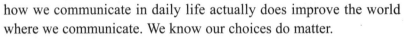 how we communicate in daily life actually does improve the world where we communicate. We know our choices do matter.

An awareness that all life on earth is interconnected changes our thinking about the nature of the universe, the nature of God and the nature of our own souls. From a religious belief in our innate union with all life, we now have visible evidence of it. We advance from the Age of Faith into the Age of Knowledge.

The notion that each of us is separate and powerless is mistaken. Biology, physics, mass media, economics, politics, and history amply refute such a misconception. Our former mindmap said each of us is so isolated, weak and stupid that we need to be ruled by masters. Now we're shifting into a healthier worldview: We each are so naturally interactive, strong and intelligent that we can govern ourselves. Our power flows from sensing our global oneness.

The idea is spreading that we're all part of one Global Brain, *Gaia*, or any term you prefer for the living earth. Ross Ashby spoke of this as "cybernetics," which inspired biologist Ludwig von Bertalanffy to express interdependence as General Systems Theory, featuring open and closed systems. (Earth is a mostly closed ecosystem). A vision of life as interactive informed the mind of R. Buckminster Fuller, who designed the "geodesic" sphere and dome as an artifact of our integral "spaceship earth." Such ideas are reshaping world culture.

A global view of life is being spread by mass media. The press tells us about our interdependence in news stories on global trade, global warming, global health risks, global overpopulation, the global war on terrorism, etc. Advertising is indoctrinating us to be globalization consumers within one world marketplace that links fishing villages to farm towns to major cities. We're being taught to think globally.

Now is a trailblazing moment for humanity. The direction we go today will chart the future course of life on earth. Recognizing how local actions have global effects, we realize why Jefferson advised us, "Whenever you do a thing, act as if all the world were watching."

DEVELOPING global sense can start by realizing the nature and power of interactive communication. We need to understand how we use the communication process to make sense of our lives and our world. To comprehend our interactivity here on earth, please study my illustration of the communication cycle.*

Effective communication happens when we transfer an idea from our mind into the mind of another. This requires a *sender* and a *receiver.* Both roles are crucial. There can be no *yang* without a *yin.*

Here's how the process works:

• The sender encodes an idea into a message that the receiver can decode or understand. To encode clearly, the sender needs empathy for the receiver.

• The encoded idea is sent to the receiver through any medium, any verbal or nonverbal message channel—from speech to smoke signals, a whisper or a wink—like saying to a lifemate, "I love you."

• The receiver decodes the message to make sense of its meaning.

• The receiver may reply, encoding a return message sent by any feedback channel, such as a soft kiss. Feedback closes the loop.

• The sender decodes the receiver's reply and makes sense of its meaning. Sending another message renews the cycle.

• Background noise interferes with effective communication.

• Encoding and decoding errors cause confusion or conflict. Wars often are caused by or worsened by communication errors.

• Form and content interact. What we say and how we say it affect one another. Paraphrasing Marshall McLuhan, the medium massages the message as the message massages the medium.

---

* For an animated model, visit http://mediavisionspress.com/communication.html.

EACH thrust and response within the two-stroke communication engine affects all of those involved, to a degree, directly or indirectly. The issue is not *if* there's an effect, but *how much* of one?

Quantum physicists can show subatomic particles respond to the mental intentions of observers. This effect caused Werner Heisenberg to postulate his Uncertainty Principle, tacitly admitting the power of mind over matter. We exist in a quantum space where our minds turn waves of infinite possibility into particles of finite experience.

If thoughts are things, and things affect other things, consider the power of our words. Anthropologist Clifford Geertz said language weaves the web of every culture. *Acts of communication compose the cultures that comprise our world.* The global ecology of language and communication forms the "hoop of the world" for Native Americans or the "wheel of dharma" for Buddhists. Hollywood catchphrases like "the circle of life," "six degrees of separation" and "pay it forward" also convey our connectivity. All life is interactive.

The law of *cause and effect* governs communication and life. In Eastern philosophy, the term used is *karma*. What goes around comes around. We reap what we sow. We get back what we give out. Picture a daisy chain of interconnected karmic loops.

Our actions produce effects *by design or default*, attests business strategist Matt Taylor. Since our acts always cause an effect, we may as well act deliberately to cause as positive an effect as possible.

Thinking we can act without any consequence is crazy. What sane person leaps from a great height without a parachute or bungee cord and sings aloud while plummeting to the earth, "So far so good!"

A pebble plopped into a pond radiates ripples lapping every shore. Each act of communication reverberates outward. My rudeness to a store clerk affects how future store customers walk away and interact with others. Such acts also radiate inward. A memory of my rudeness lingers within me, affecting how I feel about myself, which affects all my relationships, including my relationship with God.

How we interact creates the society in which we interact. We each are a co-creator of reality through our daily acts of communication. We each are responsible for the global impact of our actions. We need to accept responsibility for using our global power sensibly.

ACTS of communication are how we make sense of the world and our lives within the world. Modern communication theory labels this mental process as "sense-making." How does this take place?

Our brains are designed to process information. We integrate each experience into our neural networks by coding it electrochemically into our brains. For example, mirror neurons log what we see others do as if we are doing it while the limbic system records our emotions. The human brain is a scalable, searchable data processing network for accessing all of the information we have ever stored about "reality." Each of us is a walking "intranet" in the Internet of life.

Our sense-making system contains genetic traits, life experiences and acquired knowledge. Our mental model of reality is the map and compass we use for navigation. Our *mindmap, worldview, paradigm* or *zeitgeist* organizes life for us, so new data fits into a pattern.

Without some Big Picture of how life works, even if it is mistaken, our lives do not make sense to us. We want life to make sense, so we can feel safe (thus religion flourishes). When life stops making sense, we must change how we think, or else we'll go insane.

Sense-making happens in the synapses of the brain while encoding and decoding messages and experiences. All stimuli first goes into the brain stem, the reptilian or oldest part of the human brain, which instinctively decides fight-or-flight reactions, like yanking the hand from a hot pot handle. There's a seven to ten second delay before the signal is processed by the cerebral cortex or the conscious mind.

In this sense-making process, we innately install perceptual filters to prevent sensory overload. This is healthy. Imagine hearing every sound around you in this moment at full volume.

We also construct filters to block out anything we do not want to perceive. We see what we want to see and hear what we want to hear. This is unhealthy. In *People of the Lie,* M. Scott Peck says evil results from refusing to face or admit any uncomfortable or unpleasant truth about ourselves. We place shackles upon our minds; then we deny our imprisonment. We live "in denial." I call this *split perceptions*.

I discovered split perceptions after years of being in denial about my abusive childhood. I'd repressed my anguish in the shadow of my unconscious mind, which distorted my sense-making. Only when I recognized my hidden anger did my divided self start to unify.

Split perceptions let us "compartmentalize" the mind. Witness the U.S. Presidents who looked straight into a camera and said, "I am not a crook." "I did not trade arms for hostages." "I did not have sexual relations with that woman." And more recently, "Every measure has been taken to avoid war." *Split perceptions are self deceptions.*

Split perceptions make us see life as fragmented. We think that we exist isolated and separate from other people and from all of nature. Individualism then runs amok. We abuse liberty without self restraint. We ruin our environment without remorse. We rationalize selfishness and narcissism as "situational ethics," so anything goes.

Split perceptions cause us to view life in terms of polar opposites. Natural dualism (male and female, in and out, up and down) is lost to unnatural dualism (either/or, black or white, good or evil, us or them, rule or be ruled, kill or be killed). Life seems binary for us, *Yes or No.* We cannot imagine seeing life in terms of *Both and....* We cannot see that there is no such thing as "them" because everyone is "us."

WHEN a belief system or mental map of the world fails to match reality, a creative tension results. Communication theory refers to this as "cognitive dissonance." If we do not resolve the conflict, we may suffer a neural breakdown. The trauma-drama shock to our minds can be as disabling as post-traumatic stress disorder for soldiers.

A useful term coined by author Alvin Toffler is "future shock." He described the numbing effects of ever-accelerating technological and cultural innovation in society. When the pace or complexity of change feels too mind-boggling for us to cope, people welcome a master or a savior offering simplistic answers, so life makes sense again.

Humanity has gone through major cultural shifts before. Toffler researched the *first wave* of the Agricultural Age, the *second wave* of the Industrial Age, and the *third wave* of today's Communication Age The dawning of any new age naturally causes convulsions in society. Our new epoch of global communication is one giant leap ahead for humanity greater than any footprints on the moon. Nobody on earth has ever before constructed a worldwide interactive media network. The social impact ultimately may be greater than the mastery of fire, the invention of the wheel, or the development of the modern printing press. Media theorist Marshall McLuhan predicted that this electronic network will unite humanity into one *global village.*

As we make this societal shift, even if we feel bright hope for the future and vividly imagine global thinking going global, to deny the fear we feel these days would be irrational. The attacks by terrorists and the ensuing assaults on our civil liberties are equally frightening. We're caught in the middle of a "culture war" between authoritarian and libertarian (or liberal) ideologies. Our overwhelming feelings of "culture shock" are a natural neural response.

When we feel fear, primal instincts take over. Our fight-or-flight urges are hardwired human responses to danger. In the past, we've fled to the nearest "Big Daddy" for safety. But as Viktor Frankl said, we always have the freedom to control our own minds.

If the "survival of the fittest" really means adapting to changing conditions in the right way, the wisest adaptation to globalization is to adopt global thinking and change our behavior accordingly. Why fight and die for the survival of the fittest in a world not fit for living? *Why wage wars over which master should rule us when the only sane solution is mindfully ruling ourselves?*

As global consciousness breaks the patterns of authority addiction in our neural networks, our system of protein peptides and cellular receptors changes in reply. Instead of the adrenaline rush of fear from viewing life itself as our enemy, we feel the pleasure rush of seratonin and endorphins from seeing life itself as a friend. As healthier neural patterns are enculturated into us over many generations, global sense eventually will be embedded into the DNA of humanity.

Meanwhile, until global thinking becomes an inborn trait, how can our global consciousness create the civil society we desire?

We need to exert our global power daily to generate social change. Our random acts of kindness, such as helping an elderly stranger on the road to fix a flat tire, radiates waves of love into all our relations, generating and expanding our feelings of community.

Further, by feeling connected to the whole world, a spiritual sense of oneness with all life induces a sensation of peace inside of us. We no longer need kings or other masters to make us feel safe, nor do we need to dominate others to feel secure. Liberty can thrive.

So, will fear or reason rule us today? "Where sense is wanting," wrote Franklin, "everything is wanting."

Why fear fear itself? To be free, be free.

READERS of *Common Sense* in 1776 faced the same grim panic as we face today. The secure world they had known under the crown no longer made sense for them. They felt dazed and confused. Paine's essay by this point had shown them that declaring independence from Britain made sense. But Paine still faced his greatest challenge.

He had to convince the colonists, using evidence and logic, that national revolution was practical and could succeed. If the venture was doomed from the get go, why get going? He needed to discuss the ways and means of waging war, so that hope felt real.

I face a similar challenge. I must prove, using evidence and logic, that global evolution is practical and can succeed. I need to discuss the ways and means of waging peace, so that hope feels real. The rest of this book is devoted to that purpose.

May you find here and in yourself the inspiration to take action.

New opinions are always suspected, and
usually opposed, without any other reason
but because they are not already common.
— JOHN LOCKE

16. Global Sense Counts

AS ALL men [and women] allow the measure, and vary only in their opinion of the time [when America should declare its independence from England], let us, in order to remove mistakes, take a general survey of things, and [let us] endeavor if possible to find out the very time. But we need not go far; the inquiry ceases at once, for the time hath found us. The general concurrence, the glorious union of all things prove the fact. It is not in numbers but in unity, that our great strength lies; yet our present numbers are [fully] sufficient to repel the force of all the world.

Thomas Paine was speaking of a national war, so let's update his inquiry to ask, do our present numbers suffice for world peace? How many of us alive in the world today are thinking globally and acting locally? Are our present numbers enough to have a reasonable hope of changing the course of human events? I contend global thinkers already make a difference in society, yet we need to expand our ranks and unite our strengths. Let me present the basis for my faith.

LET'S start by counting the number of global thinkers.

In the late 1990s, I researched market trends to learn that about 30 million U.S. adults (15 percent of the adult population) showed signs of global sense. I tallied numbers from direct marketing mailing lists, magazine subscriber totals, and nonprofit membership records. Those who view all life as one, ironically, were counted by tracking their niche special interests.

Who are all these separate interest groups that make up the body politic of global thinkers? Who uses global sense to guide their daily lives, from shopping habits to voting preferences? Within the United States, I've identified 12 "psychographic" population segments that exhibit awareness of our global connectivity. Here are the groups:

Categories of Global Thinkers

Human Potential Seekers	Education & Literacy Activists
Spiritual Growth Seekers	Gender Liberation Activists
Conscious Consumers	Workers' Rights Activists
Technology Futurists	Ethnic Rights Activists
Natural Capitalists	Democracy Activists
Environmentalists	Peace Activists

For a second vector, the Natural Marketing Institute and Natural Business Communications in early 2002 jointly documented that 68 million consumers in 33 percent of all U.S. households comprise a $230 billion market they called LOHAS (Lifestyles Of Health And Sustainability). They support businesses that share their commitment to natural living for their families, communities and the environment. These people purchase organic foods, holistic health remedies, hybrid cars, and other "eco-wise" products and services. The core group of LOHAS consumers is half of that, at least 30 million people.

For a third vector, turn to *The Cultural Creatives: How 50 Million People Are Changing the World*, by Paul H. Ray and Sherry Ruth Anderson. Drawing on 13 years of survey research, a sociologist and psychologist found that 50 million U.S. adults (26 percent) share the cluster of social values that I call global sense. They assert the core group is half of that number, about 25 million people.

For a fourth vector, below are my estimates on the percentages of global thinkers in eight age groups, teens to adults, based on the 2000 U.S. Census. (*=Generation Y, **=Gen. X, ***=Baby Boomers.)

Ages of U.S. Global Thinkers

Ages	2000 Population		Portion Showing Global Sense		
15-17	12 million	@	25 %	=	3.0 million*
18-19	8 million	@	25 %	=	2.0 million*
20-24	19 million	@	20 %	=	3.8 million*
25-34	40 million	@	15 %	=	6.0 million**
34-44	45 million	@	10 %	=	4.5 million**
45-54	38 million	@	15 %	=	5.7 million***
55-64	24 million	@	10 %	=	2.4 million***
65+	35 million	@	5 %	=	1.7 million
	221 million	@	15 %	=	29.1 million

Thus, 25 to 30 million American adults share a global sensibility. While still a minority in the United States, our numbers keep growing from forces like ecological disasters and government policies.

Outside of the United States, a global sensibility is most evident in the industrialized nations, especially Canada, the European Union, and such Asian-Pacific nations as Japan, Hong Kong, Australia, and New Zealand. These match the U.S. at roughly 15 percent, partly due to "Information Age" Internet penetration.

In the developing nations, poverty impedes democracy. In the old sprawling cities where colonial architecture sits under layers of soot from vehicle or factory exhaust, where children pick food scraps from festering mounds of city trash, where people feel powerless, we see a penchant for fascist regimes. Global thinking there averages at best 10 percent, highest where there's Internet access or seaports.

Bright spots in the "Second World" are South Africa (because of Nelson Mandela) and the world's most populace democracy, India (because of Mahatma Gandhi). Despite injustices yet to be reconciled and forgiven, people there have proven that social revolution can be peaceful. Keep an eye on India's neighbor, China, still authoritarian, for as India and China grow economically, the balance of power may shift from West to East. What if both lands adopt global sense?

Now let's turn to the "Third World"—a belittling epithet from the industrial "First World," which wrongly measures intelligence by the use of technology. Tribal people are the hardest hit by globalization. Given fierce genocidal "ethnic cleansing" in lands like East Timor, Rwanda or the Sudan, Third World global thinking averages 5 percent at best. (If my estimate is too low, I'll be glad.)

Taken altogether, the extent of global thinking worldwide might average about 10 percent. The UN puts planetary population at about 6 billion, and 10 percent equals *600 million global thinkers*.

Our numbers grow daily. Awakening us to our global interactivity are global media networks, corporate globalization, the global war on terrorism, global warming, global pandemics like HIV/AIDS or bird flu, to name key factors. I lament such negative reasons for becoming enlightened. And yet, as we face dark clouds menacing an apocalypse created by our authority addiction, popular illumination from global thinking may be the one silver lining in our misfortune.

ARE there enough global thinkers on earth today to tip the scales of history from war to peace, from despotism to democracy?

Malcolm Gladwell's book, *The Tipping Point*, explores the theory from Alvin Toffler that there are pivotal moments in human history when civilizations change directions. One such tipping point came in 1776 when Thomas Paine published *Common Sense.*

Social scientists say a turning point is reached when a threshold percentage of the people starts thinking a new way. Once we reach a *critical mass,* pent-up cultural pressures induce the rest of society to adopt that viewpoint. People act as if they'd never thought otherwise, as if they always knew the flat earth was round. Where is the tipping point for global sense? If it's 25-30 percent, we're getting close.

Ever hear of the *hundredth monkey phenomenon*? The story goes that a primatologist began teaching island monkeys how to wash their food at the beach before eating. When the hundredth monkey adopted the habit, all of the monkeys on the island began washing their food. Then all the monkeys on the neighboring islands (separated by shark-filled waters, of course), started washing their food, too.

Unlike that "urban legend," we have historic proof for the theory of quantum social shifts as one cultural mindmap supplants another. Note how relatively quickly Christianity replaced the Celtic religions in Europe after Emperor Constantine converted in 312 CE. Or notice how our world has changed since the advent of the public Internet in the 1990s. From globalized technology alone, if from no other forces, the social shift into a global sensibility seems inevitable.

I wish we could afford to sit back and let nature take its course, but we can't. Our survival on earth is in peril.

Perhaps the most dire threat is what Paul Ehrlich labeled as the "population bomb." From 1 billion humans on earth a century ago, we've now passed 6 billion, growing exponentially toward 12 billion. Plague, famine and war traditionally kept the population in check, but recent scientific advances enabled a population explosion, chiefly in the Third World. Without birth control, our birth rate will keep rising. Can our planet sustain the pressure of so many people?

From sources like *The Last Hours of Ancient Sunlight* by Thom Hartmann, I'm sorry to report that in the year 2000, about 13 million tons of polluting chemicals were dumped into our environment daily.

At least 100 species of plants and animals went extinct daily. About 200,000 acres of air-refreshing forests were destroyed daily. We daily lost about 200 million metric tons of the ocean plankton that supplies 70 percent of the oxygen in the earth's atmosphere. Now multiply all this daily devastation by 365 days a year. Multiply this damage by all the years that pass before we act effectively.

Each year passing without a change in our self-destructive habits (caused by our self loathing and authority addiction) is another year we move closer to an ecological point of no return. The planet may no longer support life as we've known it. Mutating microbes may survive, and probably the cockroach, but not human beings.

So, we return to the question: If global awareness is necessary for human survival, how many of us must start thinking globally before global thinking can stop our self destruction?

Compare 600 million global thinkers worldwide, or ten percent of humanity, to the one percent of us who now controls 90 percent of the earth's wealth. Global thinkers may still be short of the tipping point, but how can we keep believing there are too few of us to matter in the world? Our numbers surely suffice to awaken the six billion of us still asleep to the power of our interactivity. "It does not require a majority to prevail," said Samuel Adams, "but rather an irate, tireless minority keen to set brush fires in people's minds."

Yet there's a better, more surprising, more personal answer to the question of how many of us are enough to save the planet.

One is enough. *You* are enough. As Gandhi said, "You must be the change you wish to see in the world." The paradox is that no one else can do your growth work or community work for you, but you cannot do it alone. We need the support of others. What we do by ourselves is powerful; yet by working together, we are unstoppable.

"Never doubt for a moment," said famed anthropologist Margaret Mead, "that a small group of committed, thoughtful people can make a difference. Indeed, it's the only thing that ever has."

Let us each awaken to the light of our planetary unity and declare our rights as free souls who daily co-create our lives and communities in partnership with our Creator. Let us practice the powerful strategy of *self improvement for world improvement.* Such a shift in our thinking inevitably will transform human society. Peace, freedom and justice on earth then will become as natural for us as breathing.

In a larger sense, the battles in every land are part of one struggle: The ancient conflict between our authentic selves and our authority addiction. We face a compulsion to give away our power to others or to wield power over others. War on earth will never end so long as we consent to mortal combat inside ourselves.

If we await perfection before we practice self rule and personal democracy, entropy will kill us. "Even if you're on the right track," said Will Rogers, "you'll get run over if you just sit there."

Recall Paine's comment about looking for the right moment to act. He said our inquiry ceases at once, for the moment has found us.

Global sense is a good idea whose time has come.

Civility costs nothing, and buys everything.
— MARY WORTLEY MONTAGU

17. The Price of Peace

HAVING proven their numbers sufficed for independence, Paine had to prove America could afford to fight a revolutionary war.

> Can we but leave posterity with a settled form of government, an independent constitution... the purchase at any price will be cheap. But to expend millions for the sake of getting a few acts repealed, and routing the present ministry only is... using posterity with the utmost cruelty; because it is leaving them the great work to do.

In today's terms, if we can leave our heirs a settled form of global government, a global network of free and equal national democracies under a common social contract based on global sense, the cost will be cheap at any price. But if all we do is repeal reactionary security laws and vote out the lousy leaders, but we fail to end authoritarian thinking, our failure would cruelly abuse our descendants, leaving to them the task of self liberation we ought to do ourselves.

Let's look at the price we need to pay for world peace, starting with changes in society, then looking at changes in ourselves.

BEGIN with the economics of war.

According to Jane's Information Group, the United States spends more on military forces than all the other counties on earth combined. Most of these costs are being financed by "deficit spending," that is, by loans, which chiefly benefit only the bankers and gunsellers.

Take the U.S. war in Iraq, for example. Based on Congressional appropriations, CostofWar.com reported the price of the war through 2006 passes $315 billion, rising $75-100 billion annually, equaling about $30,000 in taxes for every U.S. household. That $315 billion spent on war in Iraq instead could have funded basic immunization of every child in the world for 90 years, or fully funded global anti-hunger efforts for ten years, or paid for 4.5 million additional pubic school teachers for one year, or built 2.5 million public housing units for the homeless. A fraction of those billions could have fully funded the proposed U.S. Department of Peace.

Debt is rarely good, but if we must saddle our heirs with debt, let it be to improve the social conditions planting the dragon's teeth of endless war. If we must go into debt, let it be for our enlightenment. Why not invest in peace? For starters, I advise investing in education, the Internet, clean energy, and generating common prosperity.

MONEY spent fighting wars and crime is far less productive than money spent on education. Project Literacy at the University of North Carolina in Chapel Hill offers disturbing statistics:

A third of all U.S. adults are functionally illiterate, unable to read at a third grade level. Half of the U.S. population never reads books. Half of the chronic unemployed are illiterate and twice as likely to be unemployed as literate people. Children of illiterate parents are twice as likely to remain illiterate as the children of literate parents.

Three out of every four jobs in America now require a high school education or beyond. Adults without a high school diploma earn 40 percent less in their lifetimes than adults with a diploma.

Illiteracy drives the poverty that drives crime. Among 2 million U.S. prison inmates (the most *per capita* of any country), 75 percent lack a high school diploma. Keeping an illiterate adult in jail costs $30,000 to $50,000 a year. Yet teaching a child to read and write costs $3,000 to $5,000 a year. *More schools means fewer prisons.*

The U.S. Government spends $15 billion annually on literacy, yet illiteracy rates keep rising. Illiteracy indirectly costs the government another $25 billion every year in unrealized income tax revenues, welfare checks and related social expenses, reports Project Literacy. Rising illiteracy costs U.S. businesses more than $60 billion annually in lost productivity. We cannot afford these costs.

Illiteracy dooms us to tyranny, said Latin American educator Paulo Freire. *To secure democracy, invest in literacy.* Develop funding for teaching youth *how* to think, not *what* to think. Every student should learn the logical syllogism and the Scientific Method. Ultimately, we need to create more educated voters with global sense. As H.G. Wells said, we're in "a race between education and catastrophe."

Let's work to reverse the growing trend of anti-intellectualism in America and other nations. The "dumbing down" of the population only serves those who wish us to be too ignorant to defy authoritarian leadership. *Ignorance is not bliss; ignorance is bondage.*

Join with Barack Obama in countering the notion that a child of color reading a book is "acting white." Support education as a natural human right, not an elite privilege of race or inherited wealth. Truly, a mind *is* a terrible thing to waste. "Genius without education," wrote Ben Franklin, "is like silver [still] in the mine."

Link the funding of local schools to the economic development of local communities. Without decent jobs as an incentive, the poor and downtrodden have scant motivation to educate themselves.

Let's connect schools and homes with digital networks to promote *distance learning* and *lifelong learning.* To cross the "digital divide" between the haves and have-nots, invest in "appropriate technology" transfers to poor areas, such as two-way Ka-band satellites, so village schools and small business ventures can go global.

"Educate and inform the whole mass of the people." proposed Jefferson, urging universal literacy. "Enlighten the people generally, and tyranny and oppressions of body and mind will vanish like evil spirits at the dawn of day."

IF THE Internet helps generate a sense of our global interactivity, then as a way to foster such *deep literacy,* let's invest the money now spent on war to accelerate construction of the global Internet.

This proposal gains force by seeing how readily the decentralized Internet evolved as a democratic "virtual" community of freethinkers. Marshall McLuhan predicted this sensation of global unity in both *The Medium is the Massage* and *The Global Village.*

For the Internet to achieve its best potential, we need to further the "megatrend" John Naisbitt described in *High Tech/High Touch,* so human sensitivity balances the sterility of silicone chips. Books like *Technopoly* by Neil Postman warn of abusing technology, yet Howard Rheingold in *Smart Mobs* contends that communication technologies amplify our talent for cooperation. Books like *Telecosm* by George Gilder, *Being Digital* by Nicholas Negroponte, *Release 2.0* by Esther Dyson, and *Cyberculture* by Pierre Levy assure us that the Internet can transform our social consciousness for the higher good.

This cultural impact of the Internet will increase with broadband convergence of the television, radio, telephone, and computer. In Tom Paine's day, an unexplored American continent fueled the dreams of colonists. The "New World" was already occupied, but in the empty electronic realms opening today, the only limits are bandwidth, digital server capacity and imagination. The undiscovered country of global Internet cyberspace has appeared for us today, like Paine wrote,

> as if the Almighty graciously meant to open a sanctuary to the persecuted in future years, when home should afford neither friendship nor safety.

Let's modify the business model for the media. Instead of network users only being content consumers, let more of us become "content creators," selling our work over the Internet and new interactive TV channels, so we can prosper in the global electronic marketplace.

Rather than being a tool for our enslavement by some Big Brother, the Internet can be our tool for self liberation and genuine freedom, just as Peter Huber imagined in *Orwell's Revenge*. The tool is neutral, like a hammer we can use to build an outhouse or a mansion. Let us choose to use the Internet as an instrument for freedom.

ANOTHER price we need to pay for peace is the cost of weaning us from fossil fuel addiction. We need energy solutions and policies that do not disturb the peace of the world. We can end the oil wars, which have plagued our planet for more than a century.

Our economic, political and social capital needs to be invested for shifting civilization to renewable energy sources, like solar and wind, hydrogen, biodiesel, biomass, geothermal, or fusion. Why battle for a scarce resource when natural abundance surrounds us?

If we convert to clean electricity instead of burning fossil fuels, for instance, we could adopt the plan at GENi.org. Electric utilities on the low-demand night side of the earth could feed surplus electricity "over the grid" to the high-demand day side of the planet. Electricity distribution could rotate as peak load travels with sunlight.

For transporting people or goods on the ground, gasoline-electric hybrid vehicles are viable until hydrogen fuel cell vehicles are cost-effective. For personal transit, ride a bicycle or a Segway scooter. For mass transit, study the magnetic-levitation train in Shanghai.

Further, we can replace almost all fossil-fuel petrochemicals with renewable biomass sources. By fermenting plant fiber, engineers can refine biodegradable plastics for diverse applications. If we invest in theoretical and applied research, who knows what's possible?

Do not drag out the transition to appease petroleum stakeholders. We may already be too late to avert devastating climate changes. The growing pace of icecap melting from global warming, for example, puts more water in the oceans and more pressure on the earth's crust. Added weight may have amplified the undersea earthquake causing the disastrous 2004 Indian Ocean tsunami. Warmer oceans also likely amplified the catastrophic force of Hurricane Katrina in 2005.

The only people today who dispute global warming are those with a vested interest in the status quo. The world needs to hear from more of us who know it's in humanity's best interest to end our dependence on fossil fuels and invest in alternative energy.

OUR best peace investment is creating prosperity for everybody. Contented people do not wage wars, the best kind of peace dividend. "Peace and friendship with all [hu]mankind is our wisest policy," wrote Jefferson, "and I wish we may be permitted to pursue it."

Currently, by default, humanity has consented to a global social contract that locks in poverty for 75 percent of us while a fraction of us claim the earth's resources as private property. We've consented to a society where prosperity seems to most of us like a futile dream.

Some advocate socialism as a solution to the disparity. The state is supposed to redistribute all wealth "equally." In my view, we need a safety net for those unable to care for themselves, yet if we reinforce codependence on welfare among capable people, we rob them of the incentive to achieve their highest potential.

We need a global commercial framework that helps the common people to thrive. We need an actual "level playing field," not mere lip service. Break up the monopolies and create open markets friendly to small businesses, as Adam Smith wanted. More micro-lending, like FINCA offers, can help local ventures be globally competitive.

A proper role for government is assuring marketplace fairness, not protecting campaign contributors. Instead of tax breaks for the rich who can afford their taxes, let's see tax breaks for those struggling to make ends meet. Instead of governments earning revenues by selling arms to oppressive regimes, let our governments earn fair taxes from exporting technologies that help nations become self sufficient. This tactic would create more friends than enemies.

Further, we need to end hunger while we improve food safety. For example, no-till organic agriculture reduces soil erosion, creates jobs, and trims health costs by reducing the environmental poisons making people sick. To gain more tillable land, try greening the deserts. Can we convert coastal oil refineries and pipelines to carry desalinated water inland? Could the arid "Fertile Crescent" bloom again as a horn of plenty to feed the world? More desalination plants would help the one billion people now living without clean drinking water.

To fund global affluence, it pays to remember that commerce is older than capitalism. We've only lately judged wealth by what we consume over what we produce. Rabbi Michael Lerner in *The Left Hand of God* says that the right champions the selfish materialism of "unrestrained capitalism" while blaming the left for the moral crises of family instability and dark loneliness caused by those commercial values. Sadly, the left stays deaf to our spiritual hunger, appealing only to our economic interests, and thus fails to win elections.

What if we instead champion sympathetic capitalism, what Adam Smith actually imagined? Let's enroll *prosperity for posterity.* Let's invest in creating the critical mass for a global shift, such as backing both corporations and nonprofits improving world conditions.

Living debt-free is good, but we go into debt for war, so why not for peace? As Franklin wrote, "Never has there been a good war or a bad peace." If our mission is to create a sustainable future, compared to the costs of endless war, the price of peace is a bargain.

BEYOND economics, each of us needs to pay a personal price for creating peace. Specifically, we need to make daily choices that make global sense. For help, let's turn to a contemporary of Thomas Paine, the moral philosopher Immanuel Kant.

Kant published his *Critique of Pure Reason* in 1781 and then *The Metaphysics of Morals* in 1785. Often compared to Plato or Descartes in his depth of thought, Kant ended the bitter philosophical turf war between rationalism and empiricism as a means of knowing the truth, Kant encouraged us to use reason *and* experience (with intuition) to make ethical choices in the world.

Kant was a global thinker, centuries ahead of his time. Inviting us to consider the worldwide consequences of our actions, Kant gave us the *Categorical Imperative*. He said an act is "morally good" if...

1. We would wish for all people everywhere to perform that action. *What if everybody...* ate organic foods, drove electric cars, or hijacked airplanes? Would it make sense if our choice was a global law?

2. The act would *treat other people fairly* as ends unto themselves, not merely as the means to our selfish ends. Whenever we view others only in terms of how we can exploit them, that's immoral.

3. The act would *treat others as our equals,* as mutual lawmakers (co-creators) in a common "realm of ends," not so the ends justify the means, but so the means justify the ends.

Kant opposed *utilitarian* morality, promoted in his time by Jeremy Bentham and later by John Stuart Mill: If moral value is measured by the pleasure or pain caused by any given action, whatever yields "the greatest happiness for the greatest number" is moral. Do you agree? If enslaving a minority makes the majority happy, is it moral?

Kant said utilitarian attitudes devalue those supposedly benefiting from our acts. Do we help feed the homeless to "do the right thing," for example, or merely to feel good about ourselves?

Kant's categorical imperative is especially helpful for examining the morality of government policies. What if *all* governments waged preemptive wars on nations that hadn't actually attacked them? What if *all* nations revoked the civil rights of citizens on the suspicion they may not act responsibly? Logically, what would be the result?

A VITAL personal price we can pay for peace is investing energy into changing how we individually resolve conflicts in our lives.

Fortunately, the principles of *peaceful conflict resolution* are well proven, even if applied too rarely. Specifics vary among approaches, yet each shares the tenet that effective communication with a positive attitude can settle any dispute. Violence is a sign of failure.

When facing a conflict, our first focus must be our own behavior. Past choices may not fit the current situation, so let's think before we react. Let's compose our minds for "active listening" with empathy to what adversaries are saying. Let's be willing to accept responsibility for our part in creating any problem. This means facing our authority addiction habits, such as always needing to be right.

The crux is turning the divisive energy of angry conflict into the unifying energy of loving peace. Among the many tools for this is the martial art of Aikido. As Thomas Crum says in *The Magic of Conflict*, we begin by feeling solid in the center of the body, which is below and behind the navel. When we anchor that one point into the earth, so we feel calmly grounded, we cannot be pushed off balance.

Once we've done our inner work to resolve a conflict peacefully, we lay a foundation for finding solutions cooperatively together.

• We begin by agreeing on communication rules, like no yelling, blaming, name-calling, or interrupting one another when speaking. We agree to attack the problem, not the other person.

• All parties then agree to share their views calmly, perhaps with a facilitator or mediator ensuring they hear each other clearly.

• Next, find common interests among those in the dispute, if only a mutual wish to "save face," to look good to friends and allies.

• Build on shared interests to create options. Brainstorm possible solutions. Let ideas surface without acceptance or rejection.

• Evaluate the options together, looking for usable answers to real problems, voicing thoughts and feelings in a respectful manner.

• Be willing to take a brief "time out" when anger arises, then come back with a renewed determination to seek fair solutions.

• Negotiate agreements on easy points, then build into agreements on the more difficult points. Where necessary, agree to disagree.

• Make sure any deal maintains a stable balance of powers among all parties, which may mean a tangible or symbolic exchange.

• Set up ways to verify compliance with the deal, ways that do not rely on aggression. Think ahead. Plan for contingencies.

• State the agreement in an understandable form, perhaps written, and affirm the agreement, if suitable, with a ritual or ceremony.

These principles can apply to any kind of conflict that may arise in our homes, schools, workplaces, communities, or nations. Imagine the benefits in relations among nations, races and religions. All of this comes down to how we treat other people, effective human relations, such as taught by authors like Dale Carnegie.

Pioneering psychologist Carl Rogers' classic book, *On Becoming a Person,* presented his questions for forming "helping" relationships: Can I be dependably real with other people? Can I let myself feel a positive attitude toward other people? Can I enter the world of other people's feelings and see the world through their eyes? Can I separate my feelings or needs from those of other people, so I don't fear losing myself? Can I accept all facets of other people unconditionally? Can I drop my judgments about other people's life stories and see them as in the process of *becoming* their authentic selves?

Rogers cited Martin Buber about the value and the power of seeing people as "capable of inner development." When we forgive people's past faults and hold a vision of them that invites them to be real with us now, we empower them to be their highest and best selves.

THE greatest personal price to create a world of peace needs to be paid by men. We men need to give up our compulsion to dominate society and to create a world of war. We need to let go of our primal addiction to fighting one another for alpha male rule.

Since before the rise of male rule at the dawn of the Agricultural Age (or before), we men have been the guardians of women, children and property. Over thousands of years, our defensive skills have been distorted until aggression and violence are central to our masculine identity. We falsely think we must conquer other men (or corporations or nations) for us to have any value in society.

In men's suppression of women—such as during the European "witch hunts" in the Middle Ages, which killed millions of women in a Christian war against the Celtic goddess nature religions—we men suppress our feminine traits. We lose access to the broad range of our emotions. In plain terms, we close our hearts. We choose to live from our necks up and from our groins down.

Today's man still has a natural warrior inside waiting to give him the power to lead a creative life of integrity and love. This is why we men need to stop being callous soldiers serving tyrants or kings and instead become peaceful warriors serving all of humanity.

To make the shift, we men need to face the repressed hurt feelings driving us to brutality. We need to own our destructive, unconscious shadow selves. We need to befriend fear. We need to acknowledge the "Wild Man" inside, as Robert Bly said, lifting up the "Golden Child" buried beneath our darkest pain. We need to change "male bonding" from sports and beers into supporting one another in living from our hearts. We need to take women off their pedestals and see them as our equals. This is the cost of freedom from our addiction to war.

Although we men conceal more shame inside than do women, we have lots of help available to us. The ManKind Project, for example, offers initiation into authentic manhood. We men also can reclaim our true power through such "men's liberation" teachers as David Deida, Warren Farrell, Robert Glover, Herb Goldberg, Robert A. Johnson, Daniel Levinson, Robert Moore, Malidoma Somé, and others.

We men need to break the addictive cycle of violence. Whenever a conflict arises and our aggressive impulses build up, instead of an explosion followed by remorse and a period of calm before the cycle starts over again, we need to stop and think before we react. We need to relent when fear is driving us. We need to pray for serenity. A man needs to express his feminine *yin* side to be whole. A man who denies vulnerable emotions like sadness, who cannot cry, is only half a man. When men find peace, the world will find peace.

I was indoctrinated as a youth to believe that being a man means to be in total control. I was told that giving up power meant being less of a man. I was told a man should be bossy and take what he wants. Through my studies of Taoism, however, I've realized that the nature of masculine *yang* energy is not taking but *giving*. Therefore, the true character of a good man is generosity.

Rather than fighting to get my needs met, rather than acting from a place of scarcity, afraid of never having enough or never being good enough, as I release my shame and trust that my generosity stimulates the universal flow of fertile energy, my needs get met. By living with a giving heart (if I avoid codependent caretaking), my personal and business relationships blossom with abundance and sweet joy. My life works best when I open my heart. The more I open the faucet to God's infinite flow, as Eric Butterworth suggests, the better my life works. The more I erase my fear of inadequacy, the more compassion I feel for others, and the more my own needs get met.

When both men and women feel willing to pay the personal price to shift from making war to making peace, if only in our corner of the globe, if only just for today, the whole world changes in reply.

Imagination! who can sing thy force?
— PHILLIS WHEATLEY

18. Practical Idealism

WHAT is the secret for translating the global ideals in our minds into local realities in our daily lives? Thomas Paine gave an important clue in his 18th century bestseller, *The Rights of Man*.

> The danger to which the success of revolutions is most exposed, is that of attempting them before the principles on which they proceed, and the advantages to result from them, are sufficiently seen and understood.

Deep power dwells in the distance between vision and action. In *The Path of Least Resistance,* Robert Fritz urges us to squarely face the facts of our current reality. At the same time, he suggests, vividly imagine the reality that we want instead. As we amplify the creative tension of cognitive dissonance, we migrate one decision at a time from the reality we dislike into the reality we desire. When we reach our goal, we look back and call our progress a miracle.

The miracle can happen once we accept ownership of our global power in our interdependent world. The tiny changes we make in our behavior today will forever change our lives and our world.

Some of the changes caused by our actions may be dramatic, like the *New York Times* reporter who broke the news that President Bush had approved illegal wiretapping of U.S. citizens, triggering calls for impeachment. But cultural change usually emerges over many years. Observe the gradual adoption of democracy on the planet since 1776, or the long trek by women toward equal rights in society.

The strategy of people changing the world by changing themselves is not new; it just needs reviving. We need a catchphrase to popularize the strategy, so let's embrace the term, *practical idealism.*

It's much easier to declare abstract principles than offer concrete examples. As a start, among the many ways we can affect our world, let's look at how we *live, love, learn, work, play, pray,* and *vote.*

LIVE. How well do we care for the bodies keeping us alive? Are we making lifestyle choices that support our global values?

At the most primal level, what we eat affects global ecosystems and tips the balance of world economic power. For proof, read books like *Diet for a New America by* John Robbins, *Diet for a Small Planet* by Frances Moore Lappé, *Mad Cowboy* by Howard Lyman, and *Stolen Harvest* by Dr. Vandana Shiva. Our food purchases are votes.

How well do we maintain the health of our bodies? The "obscenity of obesity" in the United States costs billions of dollars to treat heart disease and diabetes. If we'd eat right and exercise more, the money spent on surgery or drugs instead could support wholistic health care research, so we could enjoy longer, more productive lives.

Whether we live in a land with universal health care, like Canada, or in a nation with private health insurance ,like the United States, if we practice wellness principles, we lower health costs for everyone, including government, so health care is more available to all.

We need to see health care as a natural right, not as a profit center. The high cost of medicine is due to marketing and insurance far more than research. The drug companies study treating symptoms, such as headaches, more than finding causes, like learning what "dis-ease" a headache may be signaling. Meanwhile, a third of humanity (mostly in poor nations) now has Tuberculosis, curable with $3 billion a year. HIV/AIDS killed 8,000 people daily in 2005 with half of all cases in Africa, yet only one percent of the global AIDS funding reaches that continent. Clearly, we need to lobby for health justice.

How about our lifestyles? In our consumption of household goods, do we *reduce, reuse* and *recycle* paper, plastics, metals, glass? Is our home energy efficient? Do we turn off lights as we leave a room? Do we conserve water? Do we drive an eco-wise car? Are we "conscious consumers" who buy products that uphold our values? Voltaire wrote, "The safest course is to do nothing against one's conscience. With this secret, we can enjoy life and have no fear from death."

LOVE. Personal democracy enhances our love relationships.

Ms. Gloria Steinem advocates a cultural "revolution from within." Let's promote both female *and* male liberation. Women can't be free from gender traps until men are free from gender traps.

Fellow men, let's stop seeing women as sex objects. Women, stop seeing men as success objects. Men, stop needing sex to feel secure. Women, stop selling sex for security. Men, stop trying to be a king to feel safe. Women, stop trying to marry a king to feel safe.

The social contract of males owning females' wombs is voided by contraception and legal abortion. If you oppose either or both on the moral grounds that "all life is sacred," do your values likewise oppose capital punishment and war? Do you work to end poverty? Do you act to save our environment? If not, whether you're a man or woman, is it possible your opposition is a ploy to maintain male rule?

Given test-tube babies or perhaps cloning, is a male's contribution still needed? Men today feel as emasculated as in mythic Eden. Small wonder that modern men wage wars to prove our virility.

We need a new social contract between Adam and Eve. I propose a marriage of equal partners. If the family is the core unit of society, if couples of any gender form healthy relationships and raise children with global sense, we can stop tyranny and war on earth.

We need to outgrow codependent caretaking and "love addiction." Let's change dysfunctional habits into healthier ones. For me, rather than feeling that being with any woman is better than being alone, or that feeling enmeshed is the same as being in love, I'm committed to feeling whole within myself. I'm accepting that being interdependent in a balanced way enhances all of my relationships.

Rather than blaming my partner for problems in our relationship, I'm willing to see my part in our problems. Rather than perpetuating unhealthy behaviors from my family-of-origin, I'm doing the growth work to break those patterns, so I can love more mindfully.

Do not confuse intimacy with sexuality. Are you emotionally and spiritually present with your partner, whether making love or making dinner? Slow down to create sacred space between you. Sit facing one another, for example, gazing into one another's eyes, matching your breathing. Ask each other for permission before touching. Honoring the right to say *No* reinforces the ownership of our bodies. This is vital if your partner or yourself is a survivor of abuse, yet such respect helps any couple build more trust into their union.

Practicing personal democracy in our love life will empower us for practicing personal democracy in civic life. One of the ways we can do this is to exert our power as consumers. In the realm of music, for instance, note the harm we do by purchasing codependent love songs with lyrics saying, "I'm nothing without you." Let's be careful about the media messages we put into our collective brains.

A related step that both men and women can take is lobbying mass media to stop portraying all men as hunks or fools, to stop the constant male bashing. The media finally presents better female role models, so let's demand better male role models. Tell media execs that "men's health" is more than big muscles and prostate testing. Tell Hollywood that violence no longer is a manly solution., that we want to see good men displaying the courage of compassion. Our activism, if only one phone call or email a month, really does help change society.

LEARN. Lifelong learning may be one of the best things we can do for democracy. Make it a point to learn something new every day, no matter how minuscule. "Learning is not attained by chance," wrote Abigail Adams, "it must be sought for with ardor and diligence."

First, let's learn how to learn. To improve our sense-making, study Howard Gardner's research into multiple intelligences. Examine Mel Levine's work on learning differences and social cognition. Look into Thom Hartmann's writings on the effect of attention deficit disorders (ADD); study how diet affects learning and behavior. Balance linear and lateral thinking, as Edward de Bono advocates.

Francis Bacon said, "Knowledge is power." We need to defend our uncensored access to information without state monitoring. Lobby lawmakers to support free inquiry in schools, libraries, bookstores, or online. By learning how to think for ourselves, we refute groupthink conformity. "Doubt is not a pleasant condition," wrote Voltaire, "but certainty is an absurd one." Work to *deregulate thinking*.

Protest efforts in tax-funded schools to teach only "politically correct" ideas. Urge exploring all sides of controversial issues, like evolution vs. "intelligent design" (which are *not* mutually exclusive). "To compel a man to furnish funds for the propagation of ideas he disbelieves and abhors is sinful and tyrannical," Jefferson said.

Next, help youth prepare for adult life. Lobby educators to enrich classes in language, math, science, and creative arts. Demand more "life skills" classes in nonviolent communication, family dynamics and personal finances. Go beyond lobbying. Volunteer in your local schools as a mentor, tutor or aide. Share what you know.

And as already advised, support funding for literacy programs and distance learning. By promoting general enlightenment, we can help humanity become educated enough for democracy to work.

WORK. We can reap the harvest of practical idealism from what we choose to do for a living and how mindfully we do it.

We have a natural right to be true to ourselves in our jobs, but are we being our true selves at work? Ask yourself, am I earning a living doing work I'd do for free? If money were no object, what would I do in daily life? Not what would I buy, but what would I *do*? Do I live to work, or do I work to live?"

Marsha Sinatar counseled, "Do what you love; the money will follow." This is true, *if* we do it well and *if* we don't give up.

First of all, we need to look at our relationship with money itself. If under-earning or over-spending is a chronic habit, can we learn to live within our means? Owing is not owning, and having is not being. Net worth is not self worth. Does conspicuous consumption harm our souls and our planet? Ponder the virtues of *voluntary simplicity.*

Next, cultivate excellent work habits. If you are a streetsweeper, said Martin Luther King, be the best streetsweeper you can be. We can feel clean pride for any job done right and true.

In any job we do, are we paid what we are worth? This is my issue. Because of low self esteem, feeling lucky if anyone wanted me, I've too often accepted less pay than my peers for such work as freelance writing, media consulting, classroom teaching, or delivering a speech. As I've felt better about myself in recent years, not only am I more selective in the work I accept, I'm more confident in asking to be paid at prevailing market rates. What about you? Hoping to get rich quick is a fool's fantasy. Have patience for incremental growth.

Locke said that the fruits of labor belong to the laborer. Under the law of supply and demand, a fair chance to market our labor at a fair price is our natural right. Oppose workplace discrimination based on gender, age, race, religion, or politics. To stop worker exploitation, we may need to join or organize labor unions, perhaps global unions. If we do, let's work to keep our unions free of corruption.

With or without unions, we need to support workplace democracy. All the research since the 1930's Hawthorne Studies has proven that "participatory management" generates far greater productivity than authoritarian management. *Theory Y* does work better than *Theory X*. If we have a fair say in the work rules governing our jobs, we can feel ownership for those rules, so we feel willing to uphold them.

Advocating workplace democracy might be the most scary action I'm proposing. If we lose our jobs by speaking up for our rights, if we are one paycheck away from being homeless, the risk is huge. Yet if corporations are the last bastions of monarchy, can we stay silent?

PLAY. "Work hard and play hard," is a popular anthem. "Men tire themselves in pursuit of rest," wrote Laurence Sterne. What men and women really need is relaxation. Playtime is for self renewal.

Let's think about recreation as re-creation with our co-Creator. A quiet walk in a forest, for example, helps us feel one with nature. In communing with nature, the goal is feeling inner peace. Yet we need to find ways to be in the great outdoors that bolster our global values. Mourn for mountain meadows rutted by sports utility vehicles.

Do we play sports for fitness and the development of character? If yes, great, but what if we're an idle sports fan? Celebrating athletic excellence is worthy, but what does the merit of an athlete have to do with our own merit? Why live vicariously through surrogates?

Sports is a subset of Entertainment, our cultural drug-of-choice. We need to stop treating mass media as the *soma* that soothes us into mindless compliance in our brave new world. Roman emperors used "bread and circuses" to distract the *vox populi* from decrying gross government abuses. Why let this happen today?

To make our play safer and healthier, boycott gratuitous violence. Stop paying for sports, movies or video games promoting mayhem. When ferocity levels must constantly keep rising to keep feeding our ever-growing cravings for an adrenaline rush, we're addicted.

Further, instead of perpetuating the win/lose attitudes of male-rule competition, let's organize cooperative forms of play where everyone wins. Such fun opens up our hearts. For options, search the Web for "non-competitive," "win/win" or "team-building" games that can be adapted to any age group.

Finally, trust the rejuvenating power of creative play through the fine arts, like writing, singing, dancing, acting, painting, or sculpting. Creating art is good for our souls and helps maintain our sanity.

PRAY. If we can sustain a good relationship with our Creator, we promote good relationships with ourselves and with others. Enjoying as little as five minutes twice a day for talking with God in prayer or listening to God in meditation can attune us to universal harmony. We thereby boost our resilience to cope with life's challenges.

Self rule and personal democracy spring from a global sense of our cosmic oneness. A sure route to this awareness is *mindfulness.*

Mindfulness flows from forming the intention and cultivating the practice of paying attention to the present moment. Rather than being obsessed with the past or future, we live in the here and now. Gently watching ourselves breathe is a way to start, as practiced in eastern meditation. Or we can walk slowly in nature, feeling every footstep. *Conscious of being conscious, we can sense our global unity.*

Please invest time reading books on moral mindfulness. Examples include *The Art of Mindful Living* by Thich Nhat Hanh, *The Courage to Be Happy* by Sylvia Boorstein, *Wherever You Go, There You Are* by Jon Kabat-Zinn, and *The Power of Now* by Eckhart Tolle. Thomas Paine himself remarked in *The Age of Reason,*

> Any person, who has made observations on the state and progress of the human mind, by observing his [or her] own, can not but have observed, that there are two distinct classes of what are called Thoughts; those that we produce in ourselves by reflection and the act of thinking, and those that bolt into the mind of their own accord. I have always made it a rule to treat those voluntary visitors with civility, taking care to examine, as well as I was able, if they were worth entertaining.

How do we discern the difference between the inner voice of God and the voice of our addictive impulsivity? If the emotional energy of a message feels calm or peaceful, if it resonates in us like a clear bell, it's likely inspired by our Higher Power. If a message feels agitated, angry, jarring, or confusing, it's likely from our shadow.

Paine said that moral knowledge exists in everyone's conscience. If we each connect within to the same Eternal Source of Wisdom, we will reach similar answers to life's problems, even with the personal variations that make life on earth distinct and fertile. As Robert Persig discussed in *Zen and the Art of Motorcycle Maintenance*. We may not use the same terms to describe it, but we all know "quality" when we see it. We each have an inner sense of what is good.

If you're an atheist or agnostic who doubts God exists or guides us, to test the morality of any choice, apply the Scientific Method or use Kant's categorical imperative. Reasoning from the premise of our global interactivity is bound to yield mindful moral choices.

The more we practice mindfulness, the easier it gets to know from within what is right. Instead of codependently relying on some smug authority to tell us what's moral, we can choose from within a path in life that makes global sense. We can change our world for the better. Perhaps the best benefit of such mindfulness is inner peace.

We can explore any spiritual path to find sages teaching the peace that passes all understanding, the inner peace generating world peace. Francis of Assisi teaches us to be a channel of God's peace. Brother Lawrence teaches us how to practice the presence of God. Isaac Luria teaches us luminous joy. Ram Dass teaches us to be here now. Black Elk teaches us holiness. The are as many spiritual teachers as students willing to learn. When the student is ready, the teacher appears.

Connecting to God, as we perceive God, helps us feel secure and peaceful. From the stillpoint inside, with self restraint and a loving heart, we *balance safety and liberty.* At peace in ourselves, we live in peace on earth. We live and let live. We live free responsibly.

VOTE. Jefferson imagined a free, educated population engaged in self government. Sadly, many voters in the United States and other nations are too under-educated to vote intelligently. Even if we are highly educated, we often lack the facts to vote sagely.

Many of us do not vote at all. We believe our votes do not count. We think big money controls all elections. We think the vote is rigged. We figure, why bother? Feeling powerless induces apathy.

If we don't vote, we abdicate our right to gripe about government abuses, yet complaining about government without fixing it is absurd. *A citizenry that gives up the rights of citizenship invites tyranny.*

What if we hate state corruption and refuse to vote in protest? Too many people in too many lands have died for the right to vote. Too many people still die trying to vote. We need to honor their sacrifice and welcome our civic duty. Voting preserves democracy.

If we *can* vote, let's do our homework before we vote. Go beyond the headlines. Seek alternative news sources outside the mainstream. Visit TomPaine.com, RadioPower.org, MediaMatters.org, FAIR.org, or Reason.com. On radio or TV, tune in *Democracy Now,* Free Speech TV, Air America, Pacifica Radio, NPR, or PBS. Think critically about whatever you read and hear. Opinions and gossip are not facts. Reject anything false. Make up your own mind, then go vote.

Vote your conscience, not your cynicism. Vote for candidates who sense our global oneness. Vote for laws that make global sense.

Want to do more than vote? Become an activist, paid or volunteer. Work to register new voters. Help to get out the vote on election day. Work for publicly funded elections with equal media time for every candidate and issue. Support the development of foolproof electronic and Internet voting for direct democracy.

Want to do even more? Run for public office. Good character still matters more in politics than foxy marketing. And if elected, you can practice principled servant leadership and lead by example.

Yet if you do nothing else, vote in the next election. Your one vote may decide a close race in your town, which affects your state or your province, which affects your nation and our world. If we do not vote, as Voltaire said, we are guilty of all the good we did not do.

CHANGING how we *live, love, learn, work, play, pray,* and *vote* is not easy, but changing ourselves will change our world.

"I like the dreams of the future better than the history of the past," wrote Jefferson. To make our dreams come true, we need to bring our highest ideals down to earth where we can use them. Seek progress not perfection. *Persistence and patience justify labor and hope.*

Authoritarian ideas rule the sense-making for too many of us. When we find ourselves in troubled waters, we cling to hereditary beliefs like life preservers tied to a sinking ship. Why be pulled down to our doom? Let our minds break free! All of us are liberated when any one of us says "No!" to a dogmatic way of life.

If humanity is to survive, our addiction to authority sooner or later must end. We cannot look forward with pleasure to the prospect of humanity forever being enthralled by kings and other masters. We can feel no joy knowing each generation faces emotional enslavement. We need to visualize a better world and work for it.

To change our world for the better, we need to do what we can on our own, and we need to join with others to expand our influence. We need to know that small improvements over time build incrementally into a quantum social shift. Every act matters. To change our world for the better, we need to do what we know inside is right.

Do not give up. Do not give in. Do not give out.

The process of personal and social transformation is not easy, but because of our natural interactivity, all changes in our daily lives can and will have global effects. I still have lots to learn, but if I can grow through global thinking, so can you. If we join others to work for real democracy and lasting peace on earth, just imagine what we can do. Never underestimate our power to change the world.

There's an old saying that one raindrop joining with many other raindrops creates a flood. I will add, one snowflake joining with many other snowflakes creates an avalanche. One voice joining with many other voices creates a convincing chorus for change.

"To put the world right in order," wrote Confucius, "we must first put the nation in order; to put the nation in order, we must first put the family in order; to put the family in order, we must first cultivate our personal life; we must first set our hearts right."

Why shirk the hard work of freedom? Diderot wrote, "There is no moral precept that does not have something inconvenient about it."

Paine observed in *The American Crisis*,

> "Tyranny, like hell, is not easily conquered; yet we have this consolation with us, that the harder the conflict, the more glorious the triumph. What we obtain too cheap, we esteem too lightly; it is dearness only that gives everything its value.... It would be strange indeed if so celestial an article as Freedom should not be highly rated."

> *On the road from the City of Skepticism,*
> *I had to pass through the Valley of Ambiguity.*
> – ADAM SMITH

19. Hints for Global Democracy

OUR acts create our society, so we need a vision of the society we want to create. Given trends toward one world government under corporate control, for globalization instead to generate worldwide democracy, we need a practical plan that ensures our freedom.

Thomas Paine proposed his plan for governance of the new nation in Part III of *Common Sense*. In this update, here in Part IV feels like the best place to discuss the issue of global governance. The topic is risky, for we duly dread a global superstate. Because progressives and libertarians lack a shared vision of global democracy as an alternative to corporate control of our planet, I hope to start a conversation.

> Wherefore, as an opening into that business I offer the following hints; at the same time modestly affirming, that I have no other opinion of them myself, than that they may be the means of giving rise to something better.

Paine urged America to declare independence from Britain; then he proposed that a "continental assembly" draft the new constitution. The assembly president would be chosen by lot, rotating among the states. To keep laws few but worthy, a *three-fifths majority vote* would ensure all laws served the public good. Drafting a constitution for the new nation would be politically delicate, so he counseled forming an

> intermediate [elected] body between the governed and the governors, between the congress and the people.... Let their business be to frame a Continental Charter... Thus will be united the two grand principles of business: Knowledge and Power.... And the whole, being empowered by the people, will have a truly legal authority....
>
> [The charter's purpose will be] securing freedom and property... and above all things the free exercise of religion, according to the dictates of conscience.

Once the charter was written, which could take years to do, Paine said the intermediate conference must be dissolved and replaced by a permanent congress. In principle, *the assembly writing the charter for any new government must never continue as a self-perpetuating body of power within that new government.*

The Continental Congress closely followed Paine's plan. Jefferson drafted a declaration of independence for the 13 colonies south of the St. Lawrence River, approved July 4, 1776, which left Canada and the "wilderness" to the British. After seven grueling years of guerrilla war, with help from France, America won its independence.

The Continental Congress in 1787 adopted the U.S. Constitution. Passage hung on a compromise allowing Southern slavery for blacks in trade for the Bill of Rights for whites—a schism later causing the Civil War. These first ten amendments to the Constitution, for most of us, are what make America great. A bill of rights and responsibilities regulating individuals, markets and governments might be the only thing that protects us from tyranny in any nation.

As Paine had suggested, after the Constitution was ratified by the colonies, the Continental Congress was dissolved and replaced by the bicameral U.S. Congress. George Washington, who'd earlier refused to be America's king, accepted election as the first president.

SOMEDAY, *if* we ever manifest enough global sense to attempt world governance without perverting it into a global tyranny, we could copy Paine's "hints" for America to establish a government of equal national democracies under a world constitution.

To start, we could elect a global constitutional body with delegates from all lands, representing the broadest spectrum of humanity.* The United Nations could conduct the election, but the assembly must be independent from all politically appointed delegates to the UN.

A global social contract has never been attempted, so let this body take years to deliberate. Any constitution we invent to govern global civilization will define the rules of living for centuries. It will affect every lifeform on earth, so we must proceed carefully.

For those accepting this challenge, I will repeat Paine's quote from *On Virtue and Rewards* by Giacinto Dragonetti: "The science of the politician, consists in fixing the true point of happiness and freedom.

---

* The global Bahai community models a way of forming such a world congress.

Those men [and women] would deserve the gratitude of ages, who should discover a mode of government that contained the greatest sum of individual happiness, with the least national expense."

Once the constitution is drafted, put the new charter to a vote in a global referendum. If it fails, revise it and vote again. Repeat until it's approved. Then dissolve the drafting assembly, with deserving praise, and hail the seating of the first elected world congress, whose duty is our peace, prosperity and freedom, so help them God. Amen.

The primary political barrier to creating a just system for global governance, I suspect, will be vigorous opposition by national leaders in the defense of sovereignty. This is why the UN is so weak.

The same leaders preaching about national sovereignty, however, are vassals of the World Trade Organization, International Monetary Fund, World Bank, and other bodies never elected by anyone, bodies that deny any vote by common people on their policies. Our national governments regulate local affairs under treaties with these bodies. As the people so ruled, we suffer from *regulation without representation*. This injury is akin to "taxation without representation," the abuse of natural law that made the American colonies rebel against England.

Saying they defend us, our leaders instead betray us to a corporate superstate. Therefore, please view any furor over national sovereignty as a pretext for protecting our overlords' grasp on power.

WHAT will be the terms of our global constitution?

A true direct democracy on a global scale is not realistic, not yet. An interim option may be what I call a *direct republic.*

In a direct republic, an elected representative body writes laws for ratification by direct votes of the people. To be practical, the global congress ought to refer only major laws or policy shifts to the world citizenry for a final vote. Institute "instant runoff" preference voting for multiple candidates and rival ballot questions. To keep global laws few but worthy, consider the benefits of requiring a two-thirds or even three-fifths majority vote for global ratification.

Along with ballot referendums from the congress, the right of the people to initiate legislation or redress grievances through petitioning must be judged sacrosanct. So ballot access is not controlled by those with deep pockets, as it is now, enact "truth in petitioning" laws, and consider unpaid petition carriers. Leave no room for trickery.

To guard against elected legislators forming private interests apart from the people, *remove all private money from our public elections.* Mandate publicly funded elections. Require equal media exposure for candidates and all sides on ballot issues, as the U.S. Fairness Doctrine once required. Good pay and benefits will draw the best candidates, offsetting a vital lifetime ban on all corrupting gifts and jobs.

Let the world congress be elected by *proportional representation,* a good idea for all elected assemblies. Instead of "winner-take-all" elections, if 20 percent of any nation votes Green, 20 percent of its delegates in the world congress should be Green. Such fairness yields wider acceptance of new laws. Proportional representation also helps protect minority rights from the tyranny of the majority.

For a direct republic to work best, we'll need foolproof Internet voting. To ensure every vote counts, we'll need secure yet anonymous online balloting devices that give a voter-audited paper receipt before a digital vote is cast (essential for fair recounts of close races). Such technology is already being developed, but it still needs refinement. Let's invest public funds in tamper-proof voting machines.

Any attempt to form a global democracy is doomed until we can guarantee the voting public is sufficiently educated to vote mindfully. This does *not* mean allowing the media to hammer state propaganda into unthinking minds. This means we empower freethinking citizens to do their homework on candidates and issues *before* they vote.

To keep the global congress from getting too powerful, along with voter ratification, all powers of government not specified in the world constitution must be reserved to the national and local states.

If a local independence movement is being repressed by a national government fearful of losing its territory or resources, let the world congress oppose all rights abuses and support self determination. Just as people should never be forced to work for any employer, so people should not be forced to be part of any state. By the same token, if two states freely wish to unite into one, let the congress help them.

The premise for genuine democracy, locally to globally, is that the weight of power in the machinery of government belongs with the common people, not a congress (which ideally only writes unselfish legislation for our ratification), and not a president (who ideally only advises our votes in a direct republic). Giving us responsibility for approving the work of our lawmakers will help us mature.

People governed by any law possess an inalienable natural right to participate in creating the law governing them. This principle is a fundamental shift in the way we think about democracy, I realize, but such a shift in our concept of citizenship is long overdue.

WHAT legal framework will guard our freedom? The U.S. Bill of Rights and the Universal Declaration of Human Rights are fine starts, as is the International Covenant on Civil and Political Rights.

Paine advocated the natural rights of liberty, property, security, and resistance to oppression. Franklin D. Roosevelt upheld the freedom of speech, freedom to worship, freedom from want, and freedom from fear. Roosevelt also proposed an "Economic Bill of Rights." These include the right to a good education; the right to a useful job that provides for our basic needs; the right of a business or farm to trade without unfair competition from monopolies; the right to a decent home; the right to health care; the right to protection from economic fears like unemployment, sickness, accidents, or old age. Any global charter must embody such rights and protections, for as Paine said,

A firm bargain and a right reckoning make long friends.

If any rogue nation or global corporation violates our rights, let the world congress draft the warrant. A consensus by itself may bring the scoundrels to heal before trade sanctions or war harms anyone.

For pressing civil and criminal claims, including war crimes, we'll need an independent judiciary that fairly enforces the presumption of innocence, trial by jury, and equal justice under law. The World Court and International Criminal Court could evolve into that system.

FINALLY, you may well ask, where is the high king in this global government? There is none. A chairperson or president with obvious administrative and diplomatic duties will be essential. But I tell you, friend, the Almighty reigns within us and over the world, and does not bring ruin to society like kings and their puppet masters.

As Paine advised, pick a president by lot from the world congress, and rotate the presidency among nations. Presidential power must be restricted, like the UN Secretary General, who manages UN agencies yet influences world events only by diplomacy. The global president must never, I repeat, *never* be able to dictate policy in any way.

Note the principle that's critical for this system to succeed. Instead of a world president signing bills into law, *the final endorsement for global legislation must come directly from voters worldwide.* Let the wisdom of the planet prevail in decision-making on global issues. Prudence will point out the propriety of having elections often.

The risk of any person seeking the global presidency with a secret hunger to rule the world is too great to be ignored. So, limit the term of office. Ban all private gifts and corrupting promises of future jobs. Confer ample comforts in office and after, so temptations are easily resisted. Proof of corruption merits jail time and lifelong confiscation of any revenues so derived. (This rule also should apply to legislators and government officials at all levels, local to global.)

As our model, we could adopt the recovery movement's Second Tradition: "For our group purpose, there is but one ultimate authority —a loving God as expressed in our group conscience [group votes]. Our leaders are but trusted servants; they do not govern."

For those who organize and lead governments, let them seek rich personal growth through "servant leadership." Those who serve most lead best. Government *of* the people must never matter more than government *for* the people and government *by* the people.

Good government upholds self government.

PLEASE let me emphasize, again, I'm offering here only a vague outline for more capable minds to develop into a global constitution. Your ideas may be much better. I urge you to publish them.

Maybe I am foolish to propose *any* vision for global governance, but if we aim for the stars, we may at least reach the moon. Of course, some say it would take space aliens landing in UN Plaza before we'd ever achieve global democracy. Perhaps, but while I'd welcome proof of Paine's belief that we are not alone in the cosmos, I'd watch that event with mixed emotions. Why keep looking up to the heavens for salvation? The Creator of the universe has given us a natural ability for democracy and world peace. Let us claim our power now.

*Labour to keep alive in your breast that
little spark of celestial fire, called conscience.*
— GEORGE WASHINGTON

20. Seed Time of Good Habits

TOM Paine knew if America's crisis passed without a revolution, if the crown held sway, people would soon feel too absorbed in their routine lives to support any major social change. This fits us today.

> Youth is the seed time of good habits, as well in nations [or worlds] as in individuals. It might be difficult, if not impossible, to form the Continent [or the planet] into one government half a century hence.... Most nations have let slip the opportunity, and by that means have been compelled to receive laws from their conquerors, instead of making laws for themselves.

From tyrants we can expect nothing but our ruin. If secret police methods ever get entrenched in America., for instance, will anybody on earth be safe? Would life be worth living? If such a fate befalls us,

> Jealousies will be always arising; insurrections will be constantly happening; and who will go forth [with force of arms] to quell them? Who will venture his [or her] life to reduce his own countrymen to obedience?

When a government is suppressing the people to keep in power, who can join the police or military forces with a good conscience? A genuinely democratic government, answering directly to voters, can better regulate matters than any regime bent on domination.

Until we agree the governance of the world belongs in the hands of free people around the world—people educated enough to vote wisely on ratifying the laws of legislators in direct republics—we will remain in danger of being ruled by bullies. Until we mature enough to govern ourselves mindfully, we will face wretched abuses by our governments. Why remain a victim blaming a persecutor and needing a rescuer? Let us break the grip of authority addiction.

Our past choices have made the present situation desperate. If we allow chaos and violence to rule in this decade and the next, autocrats can justify their power. If we permit that calamity, when and at what terrible price will we ever again reclaim our former liberty?

For world peace, "government by the consent of the governed" must move from abstract theory to concrete reality. The sooner we have enough global sense to govern ourselves sensibly, the sooner we will let go of male rule as a path to security. The faster humanity can mature into the responsible freedom of real democracy, the faster our highest and best human potential may be fulfilled. Paine wrote,

> Like all other truths discovered by necessity, it will appear
> clearer and stronger every day. First. Because it will come
> to that, one time or other. Secondly. Because the longer it is
> delayed, the harder it will be to accomplish.

Now is the moment of choice. We may never get another chance like today for open democracy to enlighten the human mind and soul. Any hesitation now may be fatal. We already have the power to create a better world. All we lack is the political will to make it so.

Most of us wait for someone else to solve our problems for us. We are like the little frog placed into a pot of cool water over a low flame, floating placidly as the slowly rising heat boils it alive. If we do not act, we will die. Until we renounce our ancient cravings for kings and their kin, neither our lives nor our property will be safe. Humanity will stay trapped in the cauldron of endless war until we assert our rights, until we act upon our global vision of peace and freedom.

FROM ignorance, prejudice or inattention over long generations, we have inherited a horde of false beliefs. We've perpetuated the lies of authority addiction through all of our social institutions.

We've thought that strong men must rule us before we can be safe. We've believed the cultural, social, political, and military arsenal of governmental and corporate autocracy is too formidable or heavily entrenched to be stopped. Actually, its unwieldy machinery is far too dull-witted and cumbersome to stop us from changing society.

Exploiting our delusions, the "military industrial complex" would have us believe war supports economic growth. In reality, war is bad for business. A few ventures prosper at the expense of all the rest. War is anathema to fair markets and free democracies. Only peace secures prosperity. Leaders who urge wars with promises of economic gain are merely creating excuses to stay in power.

We've also believed that to defeat the cultural force of authority addiction, we'd need to confront the whole power of human tyranny all at once. We've presumed we must field a military force as large or larger than all the despots' order of battle. Such a mustering is not possible, nor should it be done, and clever rulers have exploited such "realism" to dispel every justified urge for revolution

Nothing is further from the truth than the Big Lie that there are not enough of us on earth with the global sense to defeat despotism. In fact, our ranks are rising toward a tipping point. But if our numbers were a mere fraction, we'd still be more than a match for any despot who drives us to the last resort of peaceful civil disobedience.

Granted, a king or a dictator could crush any one of us like a gnat. The swarm of us altogether, however, is enough to drive all dictators out of office, *if* we persist in our buzz for democracy. Our purchasing power alone, for example, puts every tyrant on earth at our mercy. Regardless of our gender, race, party, or religion, uniting the sinews of democracy and commerce is a good public policy, as Paine told us,

> for when our strength and our riches play into each other's
> hand, we need fear no external enemy.

We can rightly claim dominion over no one but ourselves. Guided from within by a global sense of our universal oneness, we can seek to advance the common good for our own good. When public actions are needed, like boycotting a toxic product, our whole force as citizen activists is deployed widely in the world instantly. Once informed, we act without a central command. By each of us trusting our conscience and doing what we know inside is right, we have an advantage over all the masters of society.

For those of us evolving a wholistic global sensibility, we already abound in all the power needed for self determination. Intelligence flourishes in every corner of our minds. We can find ways of solving problems as they arise. Our willpower is superior to those dependent on despots. We can feel compassion and act on it. Every day we help expand freedom, justice and peace in the world. Every day we affect mass consciousness through our thoughts, words and deeds.

The worthy leaders we need in the world look back at us in the mirror every morning. By standing up for what's right, we can fill the vacuum for moral leadership in our communities and our world.

> Our knowledge is hourly improving. Resolution is our inherent character, and courage hath never yet forsaken us. Wherefore, [given our global awareness,] what is it that we want? Why is it that we hesitate?

ANOTHER reason occurs why the present moment is better than past times for establishing on earth the cultural and political values for maturing into real democracy. Millions of us already are thinking globally. One day it may be billions. Our modest numbers now mean more opportunities exist to do satisfying "war work" in the campaign for world peace. Lots of paid and volunteer jobs stand vacant at every level of society, like staffing the local food bank or organizing a voter registration drive. We just need to step up and offer our help.

The infant status of global enlightenment now, rather than being against us, actually argues for our success as citizen activists.

> We are sufficiently numerous, and were we more so, we might be less united.

The worldwide "Aquarian conspiracy" movement for spiritual and political enlightenment, as chronicled by author Marilyn Ferguson, is united but *not* too organized. Good! Because we are power addicts, satisfying tasks we may do on our own otherwise would be job titles lavished by leaders on loyal followers. Instead, individuals thinking globally and acting locally are left free to ask: *What am I being called to do? What can I do that no one else is doing?* Whatever we do alone is enough, and yet joining with others expands our power. What other movement under heaven enjoys such an advantage as this?

SOCIAL change begins with personal and spiritual growth.

If we're wise, we'll take into our hearts the wisdom of Marianne Williamson in *Return To Love,* which Nelson Mandela quoted in his 1994 inaugural speech as the first black president of South Africa. "Our deepest fear is not that we are inadequate. Our deepest fear is that we are powerful beyond measure. It is our light, not our darkness that most frightens us.... Your playing small does not serve the world. ... And as we let our own light shine, we unconsciously give other people permission to do the same. As we are liberated from our own fears, our presence automatically liberates others."

In my case, I've long imagined a global career as an author and inspirational speaker. I cultivated my writing and teaching talents, but my fears held me back from going after my goal. For decades I wrote mainstream journalism articles that seldom pushed the envelope of conventional thinking. The nonconformist ideas evolving in my head felt too scary to express. I unconsciously believed I had to be perfect before I could dare to take a public stand. I kept playing small.

The turning point for me came with the death of my father from diabetes in January 2000, followed in March by the death of a sister from cancer, followed in February 2001 by the savage murders of an aunt and uncle in a home burglary. Dark grief lay heavy on my chest. I felt paralyzed. I suffered over my suffering.

Then one morning that winter, I realized that I really was grieving for myself. I had become like my father, a middle-aged man who had never fulfilled his dreams. So many deaths coming so close together made me see that I feared dying before I accomplished my soul work. I was like that little frog who needed to jump out of the pot before it was too late. I needed to save my life.

In the clear dawn of reality, with death hovering so near, a vibrant voice spoke within me. If I truly believe our global oneness makes us powerful, I need to claim my global power and change my life. I need to stop hiding my authentic self. I need to tell God, *"Here am I."*

The tragedy on September 11, 2001, directed my creative energies into updating *Common Sense.* Doing this sacred work, I've kept my commitment to God through eight rewrites, even through my fresh grief after my mother died from a stroke in early 2006.

In writing this book, to be in integrity with you, I've brought my shadow self into the light more than ever before. I've been the typical narcissistic American white male fixated on self gratification while hiding my blame and shame. After long years of growth work, as I've evolved global sense, with grateful joy, at last, I can stand up and say the real me is showing up in the world. I can say, at last, with tears in my eyes, that I love my whole self—just as I am.

THOMAS Paine saw the pursuit of individual freedom and social justice as a moral quest, an idea he voiced in *The Age of Reason.*

> The moral duty of man[kind] consists in imitating the moral goodness and beneficence of God manifested in the creation towards all his creatures.... Seeing, as we daily do, the goodness of God to all men [and women], it is an example calling upon all men to practice the same towards each other.... Everything of persecution and revenge between man and man, and everything of cruelty to animals, is a violation of moral duty.

In our struggle today for mindful self rule and personal democracy, how can we make moral decisions that carry us along the path to civil democracy and world peace? Many of us turn to religious scriptures for moral guidance, yet all religious fundamentalists equate morality with intolerance. We see proof of this in Judaism, Christianity, Islam, and Hinduism. This is why Paine distrusted organized religions as

> no other than human inventions set up to terrify and enslave mankind, and monopolize power and profit.

He advocated seeking the universal principles behind all religions, such as the Golden Rule, and applying these rules in our lives. In his spirit, we can look for wisdom outside of traditional religions.

Native American wisdomkeepers are one such trustworthy source of moral guidance. Voicing Toltec traditions, for instance, don Miguel Ruiz offers a certain pathway to a moral life in *The Four Agreements*: (1) Be impeccable with your word. (2) Don't take anything personally. (3) Don't make assumptions. (4) Always do your best.

A similar moral sentiment about personal honesty came from the Chericahau Apache chief, Cochise, who affirmed, "You must speak straight so that your words may go as sunlight into our hearts."

Another moral guide is the Great Law of the Iroquois, which said we need to consider the impact of every decision upon the next seven generations. Beyond teaching us the patience of delayed gratification, contemplating the long-term and global impact of our choices causes us to act more carefully. We can do things in a good way.

> **AS TO** religion, I hold it to be the indispensable duty
> of all government, to protect all conscientious professors
> thereof, and I know of no other business which govern-
> ment hath to do therewith.... I fully and conscientiously
> believe, that it is the will of the Almighty, that there
> should be diversity of religious opinions among us.

Emulating Paine in *Common Sense,* let us respect all religions, yet
we need to oppose government endorsing any religion over another.
Turning religious creeds into the law for all is the holy mission of all
zealots. Extremists on the left or right feel anyone who disagrees with
them is either stupid or evil. Such thinking invites tyranny.

Consider the logic of deists like Paine, Jefferson and Washington,
who saw the oneness of the Creator and the Created. If all that exists
is God, since we exist, we are part of God. If we are part of God, as
we evolve, God evolves. If we evolve with God, we are co-creators,
so we each share responsibility for creating the Creation.

Quantum physics tells us that our thoughts influence subatomic
patterns. By changing how we think, we change our magnetic g,
which changes what we attract into our lives. Changing our minds
changes our reality. Our minds are powerful.

If our universe is composed of vibrating strings of light refracted
into the broadband spectrum, literally and figuratively, and if all of
our lives are interconnected like a net of jewels in which every jewel
reflects every other jewel, then all of our religious arguments are like
fighting over which rays of sunshine are best.

When communion with our Creator descends into a power ritual,
spirituality and religion divide, for God and religion are not the same.
Spirituality expresses God. Religion expresses society.

Each religion is a social contract to follow some spiritual map for
reaching God. It's easier to maintain a course among others doing the
same. Yet there are as many paths up the mountain as seekers willing
to ascend. By knowing God through any single religion, we transcend
all religions. Paine expressed this in *The Age of Reason*:

> I believe in the equality of man[kind], and I believe
> that religious duties consist in doing justice, loving mercy,
> and endeavoring to make our fellow-creatures happy.

Paine asserted that religious creeds, like opinions, prove nothing. True morality arises naturally from the soul, and it cannot be imposed by any king or legislature. If any religion enacts its morality into law, turning nonbelievers into criminals, such judgmental actions mock God's unconditional love and deny our natural equality.

Paine, Rousseau and others urged separating church and state, as embodied in the U.S. Bill of Rights. They understood that organized religion and politics are like oil and water that do not mix well.

Personal spirituality and politics, on the other hand, can forge a mighty union. If the true source of our global problems are spiritual, not economic, then the solution is spiritual. This is why we need to support political efforts like the Network of Spiritual Progressives. Yet spiritual people don't need a formal organization to have a global impact. The natural law of our connectivity empowers us to shape the world daily through what we think, say and do.

Judaism advocates *tikkun olam*, perfecting or repairing the world, says Rabbi Michael Lerner in *Spirit Matters*. We have a moral duty for social action, to create a just society. I'd add that by trusting in the *still small voice* of conscience and a rational global sense of our deep interactivity to guide our daily choices, we can transform the world's cultural, economic, political, and ecological landscape.

Our personal survival and the survival of our children depend on us thinking globally and acting locally now. We cannot afford delays. As Ben Franklin advised, "One today is worth two tomorrows."

Let us imagine the better world our fears and prejudices now hide from our sight, and let us work toward that vision daily. If humanity is to survive, our addiction to authority sooner or later must end. We can't look forward with pleasure to the prospect of humanity forever being enthralled by kings and other masters. How can we feel any joy while knowing each generation faces unwitting enslavement?

Spiritual people around the earth, awake and unite! All we stand to lose are our chains. We have a world to win.

Every generation needs a new revolution.
— THOMAS JEFFERSON

21. Begin the World Anew

WE NEED a new social contract for our global village. If we use "globalization" as a means of promoting global sense, eventually we can secure genuine democracy and lasting world peace.

Now is not the first time humanity has attempted democracy. Let's profit from the mistakes of the past. The ancient Israelite republic went awry when they put kings above the law. The Greek democracy and Roman republic later went awry by concentrating power in the hands of aristocrats with a lust for war and empire. America's modern experiment in democracy is going awry for all of these reasons. Other democracies today likewise stand in peril. Heed Paine's warning:

> Immediate necessity makes many things convenient,
> which if continued would grow into oppressions. Expedi-
> ence and right are different things.... When we are planning
> for posterity, ...remember that virtue is not hereditary.

Since the advent of "free-market democracy," we have created together a society where wealth and power are so far removed from most of us that too few of us bother to vote. We have created together a system of beliefs where God is so far removed from most of us that too few of us ever connect to the Spirit alive inside us all.

We have scant reasons to feel hope for our world. We dread the terrorism war turning nuclear. We worry wartime limits on our rights and liberties may be permanent. We fear plagues may kill billions of us, or pollution will render the earth uninhabitable. We let our leaders keep us afraid as a ruse to keep themselves in power.

Some say we're poised for a global corporate tyranny. The risk is real, yet I join with seers like Jean Houston and don Miguel Ruiz who predict a quantum jump of consciousness into global enlightenment. In the long march of humanity on this pale blue dot of a planet we call home, *the evolution revolution is here.* As Thomas Paine avowed,

We have it in our power to begin the world over again....
Every day convinces us of its necessity.

Never again will we stand at such a pivotal moment in history, the moment when civilization goes global. After eons of spiritual, cultural and political preparation, humanity at last is ready for global thinking and the freedom it empowers. Now is the best season in ages to create just and enduring peace on earth, starting within ourselves.

Renounce the lie that we are too weak and powerless to make any difference in life. Whenever I stretch myself to claim my power, my fears arise to protect me from the unknown. That's natural, but it's not useful. Instead, by affirming the innate power of our global synergy, I know in my gut that my smallest actions *do* matter.

If humanity is going to mature into peaceful freedom, we need the courage to practice mindful self rule and personal democracy. A child afraid of standing will never walk, let alone ever run or dance.

Our choice to get up, stand up, speak up for what's right may scare us or look like way too much work. And yet, by design or default, our minds create our world daily. So, we need to use our minds to create a better world. We need to affirm positivity and liberty.

So, let us now offer an affirmative prayer of hope.

To begin, we honor God's presence from the east, south, west, and north, from above and below, and from within. We send a grounding cord from the base of the spine down into the center of the planet, and from the center of the head up into the heart of our galaxy.

Now, letting go with a relaxing sigh, we quietly pay attention to our breathing. We allow time to slow between our heartbeats until the velvet silence hums, until our bodies pulse with pure light. We radiate peace and love. We are one with the air. We are one eternal flame. We are waves in one ocean. We are one with the earth.

We unite with God as our creative partner, not as a king. We hear God's voice within us, guiding us to live responsibly free. We let go of male-rule competitiveness and embrace cooperation. We heal our split perceptions to see all life in unity. A global sense of our oneness empowers us to generate deep democracy and world peace.

Facing our authority addiction, we pray for the serenity to accept the things we cannot change, the courage to change the things we can, the wisdom to know the difference, and the willingness to take action.

We pray for knowledge of God's will for us and the power to carry that out. We accept life on life's terms. Letting go of guilt, shame and blame, we forgive the harm done to us and by us. We love people as they are. We love ourselves just as we are. We know we are powerless over others. We do not need to rescue others or be rescued by them. We meet our own needs. We no longer need kings to feel safe.

We now choose to use our personal growth for social change. We daily transform our homes, schools, jobs, communities, and nations by changing how we live, love, learn, work, play, pray, and vote.

Accepting globalization as a fact of life, to survive, we adapt to global interdependence by adopting healthier life choices. We see self discipline as self care. We treat our bodies and our planet as temples of the Divine. We eat wholesome foods. We conserve resources. We live simply. We seek to live in balance with all life on earth.

We daily create a better society with our money, our hands and our voices. We criticize rights abuses by both business and government, protesting in the streets if we must, yet we shall not be moved from nonviolence. We shall overcome hate with love. All we are saying, again and still, is give peace a chance.

We are now thinking globally and acting locally because mindful self rule and personal democracy make global sense. We are erasing racism and sexism because justice makes global sense. We are active in politics because democracy makes global sense. We are promoting prosperity because world peace makes global sense. We our changing our vision of life because *global sense makes common sense.*

When enough of us feel united with all life on earth, when enough of us feel God's presence in every one of us, then peace, freedom, health, and prosperity worldwide will follow as naturally as the dawn follows night. On that day of spiritual, political, cultural, and eco-logical harmony, we will claim equality with any in the universe.

Let us thank the God of our understanding for global healing now. Let us thank God for compassion, tenderness, patience, forbearance, kindness, awareness, for carrying love from age to age, for easing our fears and tears, for making us free. Let us thank God for the power of giving thanks, knowing the better world we imagine in our minds already is becoming the reality in our lives, one day at a time.

Now see it, feel it, say it, and let it go. Yes, let it be so.

IN CONCLUDING this update of *Common Sense*, with malice toward none and friendship for all, aware we have much to learn and far to grow, I'm deferring to Tom Paine for his own closing words:

> These proceedings may at first appear strange and difficult; but, like all other steps which we have already passed over, [these] will in a little time become familiar and agreeable; and until an independence [or interdependence] is declared, the continent [and world] will feel itself like a man [or woman] who continues putting off some unpleasant business from day to day, yet knows it must be done, hates to set about it, wishes it over, and is continually haunted with the thoughts of its necessity.

∞

Judge of a man by his questions
rather than by his answers.
— VOLTAIRE

About The Author

JUDAH FREED, an award-winning media and politics journalist, has published a thousand articles and columns since 1976 in dozens of local to international newspapers and magazines.

Freed's thinking was influenced by classical and modern writers across the philosophical and political spectrum who hold faith in our highest human potential for enlightenment. He earned a dual BA in journalism and communication from the University Without Walls at Loretto Heights College, then he researched communication theory in the Individualized MA program of Antioch University.

Kenneth Judah Freed published his first news story on September 8, 1976, in *The Aurora Sun* in Colorado, later writing for *Westword, The Denver Post, Rocky Mountain News* and others. Since 1992, he's reported on television and Internet for the top media trade magazines in America and Europe, pioneering coverage of interactive TV and distance learning. In 1998, *Financial Times* in the UK published his book-length report, *Opportunities in Educational Television.*

An educator and public speaker, Freed also serves as a consultant and coach for organizations and individuals. He applies global sense and communication principles to empower growth and change while increasing effectiveness and expanding prosperity.

A member of the American Society of Journalists and Authors, he's a past president of the Colorado Authors League and a director of the Colorado Independent Publishers Association. He's a graduate of the Dale Carnegie Course as well as Camp Wellstone.

A fourth generation Colorado native raised to cherish freedom in the wide open west, Freed also has lived in New York, Chicago, and Los Angeles. He now works from his simple home in Denver.

LEARN MORE ABOUT THE AUTHOR:
http://mediavisionspress.com/judahfreed.html

The real man smiles in trouble,
gathers strength from distress,
and grows brave by reflection.
— THOMAS PAINE

About Thomas Paine

THOMAS PAINE (1737-1809), an English writer and activist, is best known for his popular 1776 essay, *Common Sense*, the pivotal call for American independence and democracy.

Paine's thinking was influenced by English and French writers like Locke, Burke, Voltaire, Rousseau, and other *philosophes* in the social movement called the Enlightenment. Sponsored by Ben Franklin, he came to America in 1774. At *Pennsylvania Magazine,* he wrote about new technology and public affairs. He supported women's rights and co-founded one of the first abolitionist societies in America.

Paine published *Common Sense* on January 10, 1776. Out of 2.5 million people then living within the 13 colonies, roughly 400,000 purchased the pamphlet. Paine donated the bulk of his earnings to the Continental Army. Inspired by his essay, the confused and frightened colonists rallied behind the American Revolution, and so created the world's first modern republic. Without *Common Sense* to shift public opinion, historians agree, the rebellion likely would have failed.

During the war, Paine wrote *The American Crisis* series to sustain support for independence, starting with the line, "These are the times that try men's souls." After the war, he went to France to witness their revolution, defending its lofty ideals in *The Rights of Man,* the biggest bestseller of the 18th century. Honored at first in France, he later was jailed during the Reign of Terror. While a prisoner of conscience, he began writing *The Age of Reason,* a sharp critique of religion that won favor in Europe but yielded a backlash in the new United States.

Returning to America in 1801, finding himself a social outcast, he died eight years later in poverty and obscurity. Thomas Paine changed our world for the better. On his great shoulders others stand.

LEARN MORE ABOUT THOMAS PAINE:
http://mediavisionspress.com/tompaine.html

Major Works by Thomas Paine

Common Sense	1776, Republished 1791
The American Crisis	1776-83
Public Good	1780
The Rights of Man (I & II)	1791, 1792
The Age of Reason (I & II)	1794, 1795
Agrarian Justice	1797

Other Significant Writings by Thomas Paine

Case of the Officers of Excise	1772
African Slavery in America	1775
Liberty Tree (poem)	1775
An Occasional Letter on the Female Sex	1775
Thoughts on Defensive War	1775
A Serious Thought	1775
The Forester Letters	1776
Emancipation of Slaves	1780
The Affair of Silas Deane	1778-79
A Republican Manifesto	1791
Dissertation on First Principles of Government	1795
Letter to George Washington	1796
Religion of Deism Compared with Christian Religion	1804
The Prospect Papers	1804
Letters to the Citizens of the United States	1802-05
Liberty of the Press	1806
The Dream Interpreted (Essay on Dreams)	1807
Origin of Freemasonry	posthumously, 1810, 1818

For a complete list of Paine's writings or more information:

Please contact the Thomas Paine National Historical Association
(http://www.thomaspaine.org)

My country is the world,
and my religion is to do good.
– THOMAS PAINE

AFTERWORD
Self Rule: Our Responsibility, Our Birthright

by Dr. Vandana Shiva

ACROSS our wide world, across diverse cultures, across different economic and political contexts, a new awakening is dawning—that freedom is ours to create, that tyranny is in our hands to resist.

Judah Freed has revisited Thomas Paine's *Common Sense* for the reawakening of democracy. In India, we revisit Gandhi's "self rule" (*Hind Swaraj*) for the defense of our fundamental freedoms.

Corporate globalization is leading to the ultimate slavery—the enslavement and commodification of life, enclosure of the common natural resources that support all life. Commercial patents on life, the privatization of our water, the globalization and corporatization of our food supply are different expressions of this final enclosure.

When life is being enclosed, extinguishing life is the inevitable consequence, and defending life becomes the exercise of freedom. The right to say "no" springs from our duty to protect life on earth. The resistance to patent laws for seeds through non-cooperation (*Bija Satyagraha*) draws from our responsibility to save and share all seeds. In this duty lies the seed of freedom (*Bija Swaraj*).

The resistance to water privatization flows from our responsibility to conserve and share our precious water resources. Non-cooperation with water privatization (*Jal Satyagraha*) stands on the foundation of Water Democracy (*Jal Swaraj*).

The right to food sovereignty (*Anna Swaraj*) is also a duty to grow food without violence to the earth and to our bodies. Saying "no" to agrichemicals and GMOs means saying "yes" to organic foods.

In these everyday acts of eating and drinking, freedom is being redefined. It is the freedom to be, the freedom to live. Corporations seek their freedom to take profits through free trade imposed through the World Trade Organization (WTO) and the World Bank. "Free Trade" has become the ultimate dictatorship in which we are not free to save our own seeds; biodiversity is not free to evolve; farmers are not free to grow crops; citizens are not free to eat the foods of their choice; water is not free to flow down rivers; and people are not free to access the clean water that sustains life.

People seek their freedom to live through self rule, through self organization and self empowerment. I call this reinvention of freedom "Earth Democracy." Judah Freed gifts it to us as "Global Sense."

In a trying time of global corporate control, *Global Sense* is about personal and social transformation, starting with the inner self feeling a genuine recognition of our rights and responsibilities. The book is a declaration of global interdependence based on ideas of independence rooted in Gandhi's principle of personal sovereignty.

As Gandhi said to India's imperial rulers in 1916, "You are our sovereign only so long as we consider ourselves your subjects. When we are not subjects, you are not the sovereign either. So long as it is your endeavor to control us with justice and love, we will let you do so. But if you wish to strike at us from behind, we cannot permit it. You will have to ask our opinion about the laws that concern us.

"If you make laws to keep us suppressed in a wrongful manner and without taking us into [your] confidence, these laws will merely adorn the statute books. We will never obey them. Award us for it what punishment you like, we will put up with it."

Gandhi taught us that self rule is our spiritual birthright and our moral responsibility. Self rule is the path to democracy. – VS

Dr. Vandana Shiva is a globally respected scientist, activist and author. Her books include *Stolen Harvest, Biopiracy, Water Wars, Earth Democracy,* and others. She founded the Research Foundation for Science, Technology and Ecology based in New Delhi, India. For information, please visit the foundation's website at http://www.vshiva.net.

I may disagree with what you have to say,
but I shall defend to the death your right to say it.
— VOLTAIRE

Who's Who

QUOTES by writers from the Enlightenment open each chapter in
Global Sense. Below are their names with brief biographical notes.
For more information on them, go to any library or search the Web.

ADAMS, ABIGAIL (1744-1818) – *Chapter 7*
America letter writer; wife of second U.S. President John Adams.

BURKE, EDMUND (1729-1797) – *Chapters 4, 12*
British statesman and political philosopher; born in Ireland.

DIDEROT, DENIS (1713-84) – *Chapter 15*
French writer and philosopher; Enlightenment encyclopedia publisher.

FRANKLIN, BENJAMIN (1706-1790) – *Chapter 5, Acknowledgements*
American printer, writer, scientist, inventor, entrepreneur, statesman.

JEFFERSON, THOMAS (1743-1826) – Foreword, *Chapters 6, 21, Bibliography*
American statesman, architect, writer; third U.S. President.

LOCKE, JOHN (1632-1704) – *Chapters 1, 16, Study Guide*
English political philosopher; visionary democracy advocate.

MONTAGU, MARY WORTLEY (1689-1762) – *Chapter 17*
English writer and feminist, keen observer of the aristocracy.

ROUSSEAU, JEAN JACQUES (1712-1778) – *Chapters 10, 14*
French philosopher, author, political theorist, and composer.

SMITH, ADAM (1723-1790) – *Chapter 19*
Scottish economist and moral philosopher; conceived capitalism.

VOLTAIRE – François Marie Arouet (1694-1778) – *Chapters 8, Author Bio*
French writer and playwright; a luminary of the Enlightenment.

WARREN, MERCY OTIS (1728-1814) – *Chapters 3, 13*
American Revolutionary War historian, political critic, poet.

WASHINGTON, GEORGE (1732-1799) – *Chapters 2, 11, 20*
American Revolutionary War general; first U.S. President.

WHEATLEY, PHILLIS (c. 1753-1784) – *Chapter 18*
American poet, Latin and Greek translator; a slave born in Africa.

WOLLSTONECRAFT, MARY (1759-1797) – *Chapter 9*
English writer and dissident feminist; mother of author Mary Shelly.

*I am mortified to be told that, in the
United States of America, the sale of a book can
become a subject of inquiry, and of criminal inquiry too.*
— THOMAS JEFFERSON

Bibliography

Title	Author	Page
The Prophet	Kahlil Gibran	1
Bowling Alone	Robert D. Putnam	9
Habits of the Heart	Richard Bellah, *et al.*	9
Unequal Protection	Thom Hartmann	10
Discourse on Method	René Descartes	11
Novum Organum	Francis Bacon	11
The Principia	Isaac Newton	11
Leviathan	Thomas Hobbes	11
Nineteen Eighty-Four	George Orwell	11
Ethics	Baruch Spinoza	11
Brave New World	Aldous Huxley	11
Beyond Good and Evil	Friedrich Nietzsche	11
The Prince	Niccolo Machiavelli	11
Two Treatises on Civil Government	John Locke	11
Theory X and Theory Y	Douglas McGregor	12
The Social Contract	Jean Jacques Rousseau	12
The Anatomy of Self	Takeo Doi	13
Gulliver's Travels	Jonathan Swift	21
Age of McCarthyism	Ellen W. Schrecker	23
The Collected Works	Paddy Chayefsky	24
History of English Speaking People	Winston Churchill	27
Walden	Henry David Thoreau	28
The Exception to the Rulers	Amy Goodman	28
Vietnam: A History	Stanley Karnow	29
The Palmer Raids	Edwin Palmer Hoyt	33
Vindication of the Rights of Women	Mary Wollstonecraft	33
It Can't Happen Here	Sinclair Lewis	33
Overthrow	Stephen Kinzer	33
The True Believer	Eric Hoffer	40
The Chalice and the Blade	Riane Eisler	41
Bulfinch's Mythology (Mabinogeon)	Thomas Bulfinch	42
My Life with the Chimpanzees	Jane Goodall	42
Origin of Species, The Descent of Man	Charles Darwin	43
Why Men Are the Way They Are	Warren Farrell	43
The Hazards of Being Male	Herb Goldberg	43

The Myth of Male Power	Warren Farrell	43
Invisible Man	Ralph Ellison	43
The Idea of God	John Fiske	52
Nature; Self Reliance	Ralph Waldo Emerson	52
Walden; Civil Disobedience	Henry David Thoreau	52
The Course in Miracles	Found. for Inner Peace	52
Gandhi: An Autobiography	Mohandas K.Gandhi	52
A Testament of Hope	Martin Luther King, Jr.	52
Affluenza	John De Graaf, David Wann, Thomas Naylor	56
The Theory of Moral Sentiments	Adam Smith	57
The Wealth of Nations	Adam Smith	57
Das Kapital	Karl Marx	58
Unequal Protection	Thom Hartmann	59
What Would Jefferson Do?	Thom Hartmann	59
Iron John	Robert Bly	60
The Hero with a Thousand Faces	Joseph Campbell	60
The True Believer	Eric Hoffer	61
Escape From Freedom	Erich Fromm	61
Out of the Shadows	Patrick Carnes	62
7 Habits of Highly Effective People	Stephen Covey	62
Toward a Psychology of Being	Abraham Maslow	62
Facing CoDependency	Pia Mellody	63
Codependent No More	Melody Beattie	63
Games People Play	Eric Berne	63
The Undiscovered Self	Carl Jung	66
Man's Search for Meaning	Viktor Frankl	66
A Guide to Rational Living	Albert Ellis	66
Self Esteem	Caroline Myss	66
The Tao of Physics	Fritjof Capra	74
The Vintage Mencken	Alistair Cooke	74
Path of the Peaceful Warrior	Dan Millman	82
Nineteen Eighty-Four	George Orwell	82
Brave New World	Aldous Huxley	82
Walden	Henry David Thoreau	85
Theory X and Theory Y	Douglas McGregor	87
Leviathan	Thomas Hobbes	87
Self Matters	Dr. Phil McGraw	92
Civil Disobedience	Henry David Thoreau	92
Global Brain	Howard Bloom	98
Introduction to Cybernetics	W. Ross Ashby	98
General Systems Theory	Ludwig von Bertalanffy	98
Operating Manual For Spaceship Earth	R. Buckminster Fuller	98
Understanding Media	Marshall McLuhan	99

The Interpretation of Cultures	Clifford Geertz	100
Six Degrees	Duncan J. Watts	100
People of The Lie	M. Scott Peck	101
Future Shock	Alvin Toffler	102
The Third Wave	Alvin Toffler	102
War and Peace in the Global Village	Marshall McLuhan	102
Man's Search for Meaning	Viktor Frankl	103
The Cultural Creatives	Paul H. Ray	106
	Sherry R. Anderson	
The Tipping Point	Malcolm Gladwell	108
The Hundredth Monkey	Ken Keyes Jr	108
The Population Bomb	Paul Ehrlich	108
The Last Hours of Ancient Sunlight	Thom Hartmann	108
And Keep Your Powder Dry	Margaret Mead	109
Will Rogers Says	Will Rogers Memorial	110
Pedagogy of the Oppressed	Paulo Freire	112
Pedagogy of Freedom	Paulo Freire	112
The Outline of History	H.G. Wells	112
Casting the Net Over Global Learning	Bernard Luskin	113
The Medium is the Massage	Marshall McLuhan	113
Megatrends	John Naisbitt	113
High Tech/High Touch	John Naisbitt	113
Technopoly	Neil Postman	113
Smart Mobs	Howard Rheingold	113
Telecosm	George Gilder	113
Being Digital	Nicholas Negroponte	113
Release 1.0 and *Release 2.0*	Esther Dyson	113
Cyberculture	Pierre Levy	113
Orwell's Revenge	Peter Huber	114
The Left Hand of God	Michael Lerner	116
Critique of Pure Reason	Immanuel Kant	116
The Metaphysics of Morals	Immanuel Kant	116
Principles of Morals and Legislation	Jeremy Bentham	117
On Liberty	John Stuart Mill	117
The Magic of Conflict	Thomas Crum	118
How to Win Friends & Influence People	Dale Carnegie	118
On Becoming a Person	Carl Rogers	118
I and Thou	Martin Buber	119
Witches and Witch-Hunts	Wolfgang Behringer	119
Path of the Peaceful Warrior	Dan Millman	119
Iron John	Robert Bly	119
The Way of the Superior Man	David Deida	120
The New Male	Warren Farrell	120
No More Mr. Nice Guy	Dr. Robert Glover	120
The Hazards of Being Male	Herb Goldberg	120

He, She and *We*	Robert A. Johnson	120
Seasons of a Man's Life	Daniel Levinson	120
King, Warrior, Magician, Lover	Robert L. Moore	120
Ritual: Power, Healing & Community	Malidoma Somé	120
Spiritual Economics	Eric Butterworth	120
The Path of Least Resistance	Robert Fritz	121
Diet for a New America	John Robbins	122
Diet for a Small Planet	Frances Moore Lappé	122
Mad Cowboy	Howard Lyman	122
Stolen Harvest	Dr. Vandana Shiva	122
Revolution from Within	Gloria Steinem	122
Facing Love Addiction	Pia Mellody	123
Multiple Intelligences	Howard E. Gardner	123
A Mind at a Time	Mel Levine	123
Complete Guide to ADHD	Thom Hartmann	123
New Thinking for the New Millennium	Edward de Bono	123
The New Organon	Francis Bacon	123
Nonviolent Communication	Marshall Rosenberg	123
Do What You Love; The Money Will Follow	Marsha Sinatar	125
Voluntary Simplicity	Duane Elgin	125
Two Treatises on Civil Government	John Locke	125
Manufacturing Knowledge	Richard Gillespie	125
Theory X and Theory Y	Douglas McGregor	126
Tristam Shandy	Laurence Sterne	126
The Art of Mindful Living	Thich Nhat Hanh	127
The Courage to Be Happy	Sylvia Boorstein	127
Wherever You Go, There You Are	Jon Kabat-Zinn	127
The Power of Now	Eckhart Tolle	127
Zen & the Art of Motorcycle Maintenance	Robert Persig	128
The Metaphysics of Morals	Immanuel Kant	128
The Practice of the Presence of God	Brother Lawrence	128
The Zohar	Isaac Luria	128
Be Here Now	Ram Dass (R. Alpert)	128
Black Elk Speaks	John G. Neihardt	128
On Virtue and Rewards	Giacinto Dragonetti	132
The Aquarian Conspiracy	Marilyn Ferguson	140
Return To Love	Marianne Williamson	140
The Four Agreements	don Miguel Ruiz	142
Spirit Matters	Michael Lerner	144
Jump Time	Jean Houston	145
Toltec Prophesies	don Miguel Ruiz	145
Pale Blue Dot	Carl Sagan	145
The Science of Mind	Ernest Holmes	146

Reading furnishes the mind only with
materials of knowledge; it is thinking
that makes what we read ours.
                              – JOHN LOCKE

Global Sense Study Guide

NOW that you've read *Global Sense,* you may wish to discuss the book with others in a class or book club, or to discuss the book with friends. Below are questions from each chapter designed to plant seed thoughts that produce fruitful conversations. As Edmund Burke said, "Reading without reflecting is like eating without digesting."

PART I: Mindful Self Rule and Modern Republics

Chapter 1. Personal Democracy   *p. 7*
- What does "mindful self rule" and "personal democracy" mean to you in terms of your own growth as a person?
- Why did *Common Sense* make sense to the colonial Americans in 1776? Identify the main reasons for the book's popular appeal.
- Compare and contrast the philosophies of Hobbes and Spinoza with those of Locke and Rousseau. Where does Paine fit in?
- Discuss the theories of "natural law" and "natural rights" in terms of modern laws and civil liberties.
- Why did Paine say America had a right to declare independence? What does it mean for a government to become illegitimate?

Chapter 2. Origin and Rise of Government   *p. 15*
- Thomas Paine said the best form of government is the one most likely to secure our freedom at the least expense. How well does your local to national government meet this criteria?
- Discuss Paine's parable of an imaginary community going from *self rule* to a *democracy,* to a *republic, and* then sliding into tyranny. At what stage is your national government?
- Discuss any government that's decayed from freedom to tyranny. What were the cultural and political forces involved?
- How do breakdowns in communication between the people and the government tend to result in authoritarian regimes?
- What does this chapter teach regarding personal self rule?

Chapter 3. Constitutional Republics   *p. 19*
• How is the British House of Lords like the U.S. Senate? How is the House of Commons like the U.S. House of Representatives?
• Should the U.S. House vote on Supreme Court appointments?
• Discuss McCarthyism in the U.S. during the 1950s and the forces that ended it. What are the parallels to society today?
• Discuss the social and cultural impact of media "consolidation." How can we ensure that journalists report abuses of power?

Chapter 4. A House Divided Against Itself   *p. 25*
• Is a "balance of powers" in the U.S. Constitution still effective?
• Discuss Thomas Paine's machine metaphor for how government works. Do you agree or disagree with his Industrial Age analogy?
• How does our situation today compare and contrast to the fate of Charles I and the causes of the English Civil War?
• Discuss the theory that a violent revolution against any tyranny often produces another tyranny. Please cite examples.

Chapter 5. Clear and Present Dangers   *p. 29*
• Discuss Roosevelt's 1941 "four freedoms" speech. Why is each freedom important to individuals and society as a whole?
• Do you agree or disagree that the "war on terrorism" has yielded more terrorists and made the world less safe than before?
• Do you believe or doubt the official reasons given for the U.S.-led invasion and occupation of Iraq? Was the war justified?
• Do you believe the USA PATRIOT Act is unconstitutional and should be repealed? Are we unduly sacrificing liberty for security?
• Research the Alien and Sedition Acts signed in 1798 by President John Adams. Compare them to the modern Patriot Acts.
• Discuss the author's worst case and best case scenarios. What are your own best and worst case scenarios for today's crisis?

Chapter 6. Genuine Democracy   *p. 35*
• Why has no modern nation tried direct democracy? What stands in the way of genuine democracy in your country?
• Is humanity mature enough for government by the consent of the governed? What can help us become mature enough?
• Why and how is genuine democracy becoming more feasible?

PART II: Male Rule and Authority Addiction

Chapter 7. The Divine Right of Kings   *p. 39*
- Do you agree or disagree with the author's interpretation of the biblical "Fall of Man" as a myth for the rise of male rule? Why?
- Discuss Darwin's "natural selection." Does *right make might*?
- Did inbreeding taint the "royal" line of Jacob, David and Jesus?
- Does the "Promised Land" tale explain the Middle East conflict?
- Discuss the Israelites giving up the rule of law for rule by a king.
- Debate Paine's claim that the Scriptures rejected monarchy.

Chapter 8. Hereditary Succession   *p. 48*
- Discuss Paine theories on how the first kings came into power.
- Discuss the view that Jesus was an enlightened man, a "spiritual evolutionary," who's been turned into "an opiate of the masses."
- Discuss the schism of Islam into Shiites and Sunnis in a dispute over election of Mohammed's successor. Does Islamic tradition really support the election of both religious *and* civil leaders?
- How has deism influenced our modern world? When deist Tom Paine cited Scriptures to make his case, was he being a hypocrite?

Chapter 9. Inherited Wealth   *p. 55*
- Does inherited wealth help or hurt those who inherit it?
- What does using "prosperity for posterity" mean to you?
- Discuss "Affluenza." Do you suffer from chronic debting, under-earning or over-spending? If so, how do such habits affect you?
- Do you agree that Adam Smith was a social progressive? Why has capitalism ignored Smith's sympathetic moral compass?
- Discuss Jefferson's worries about the power of corporations.
- Does the name democracy still fit modern republics? In fact, can they rightly be called republics? Explain your reasoning.
- Discuss the traditions of male dominance that men inherit from their fathers. How have male myths affected your own life?

Chapter 10. Authority Addiction   *p. 61*
- Discuss the theory of *generational authority addiction* as a cause of our world's problems. Do you suffer from authority addiction?
- If humans ideally progress from dependence to independence to interdependence, how and why do we get stuck in codependence?

- What are the main social roles enacted compulsively by authority addicts? Have you enacted any of these roles? With what results?
- Would you agree that authority addiction explains our social and political urge to sacrifice liberty for security? Why or why not?

PART III: Thoughts on the State of World Affairs

Chapter 11. From Argument to Arms   *p. 69*
- Is the war on terrorism worth losing our civil liberties? Why?
- The author asks, "Why refuse to give peace a chance when peace is the only chance we've got?" What does this mean to you?
- Compare and contrast the 1775 "massacre" at Lexington with the 2001 terrorist attacks on New York and Washington, DC.

Chapter 12. Sacrifices to Superstition   *p. 73*
- Paine and the author present an array of rationalizations used by authoritarian rulers to stay in power. What are your responses?
- What do you think about leaders using emotionally loaded terms like *homeland, fatherland* or *motherland* to unite their followers?
- What are the consequences of giving in to authority addiction in our homes, schools, workplaces, communities, and nations?
- Do you agree that renouncing authority addiction is necessary for us to create real democracy and world peace? Why or why not?
- Do you believe nonviolence can defeat despotic leaders? Why?

Chapter 13. The Tyrants Last Stand   *p. 81*
- If a craving to rule the world is proof of insanity, are all would-be kings and messiahs inherently unfit for leadership?
- Discuss Göring's strategy for any government getting the people to go along with a war of conquest. Why does this strategy work?
- If it's true that tyrants always oppose any law giving liberties to the people, what can we do to assert our rights and freedoms?
- If government leaders offer to revoke the repressive security laws providing they stay in power, would you go along? Why?
- If you've gone along with a petty dictator in a job or community group, what were the consequences? Would you do it again?
- If we ever had real freedom in society, would the result be chaos? How does your reply reflect your beliefs about human nature?

Chapter 14. A Government of Our Own   *p. 89*

- The author asserts, "Global sense is *necessary and sufficient* for peace and democracy." Test the logical validity of this statement.
- If nonviolence is the best path for securing our freedom, what can you do when faced with government coercion by force or fraud?
- What would you put into a declaration of global interdependence to help yourself and humanity become free of authority addiction?

PART IV: Our Ability for Democracy and World Peace

Chapter15. Common Global Sense   *p. 97*

- Is humanity ready for global interdependence? Why or why not?
- How does our global interactivity give you the power to change the world by changing yourself? Please name examples.
- Discuss the interactive Communication Model and the process of "sense making." How does your mindmap shape your life choices?
- Can you name instances when "split perceptions" prevented you from seeing a truth about yourself, other people or a situation?
- As we enter a global age, are you suffering from "future shock"? How can global thinking help you cope with rapid social change?

Chapter 16. Global Sense Counts   *p. 105*

- The author estimates 25-30 million global thinkers in the U.S. and 600 million worldwide. Do you agree with these numbers? Why?
- Do you give credence to the *Hundredth Monkey Phenomenon?* Can you site actual examples of cultural shifts in history?
- Do you accept the idea that one person is enough to change the world? What have you done today to make a difference?

Chapter 17. The Price of Peace   *p. 111*

- The money spent on war, says the author, could be better spent for peace. How would you spend the money now going for war?
- For world peace, how would you expand prosperity for everyone on earth? What are the alternatives to top-down state socialism?
- Apply Kant's Categorical Imperative to test the morality of your government's policies for security, civil rights and other issues.
- The author says world peace depends on men being liberated from the need to rule society. What is your view of "men's liberation?"

Chapter 18. Practical Idealism   *p. 121*

- Do you believe all changes in yourself or in the world must be fast? Discuss the advantages and disadvantages of incremental change.
- Talk about how you *live, love, learn, work, play, pray,* and *vote.* Which of your daily choices make global sense? Which do not?

Chapter 19. Hints for Global Democracy   *p. 131*

- Do you believe a global constitution among sovereign nations would help or hurt humanity? Explain your reasoning.
- Would Paine's plan for writing a constitution of the United States work for writing a constitution uniting the world's democracies?
- Discuss the theory of a *direct republic* in which the legislatures draft laws and the voters have final approval (not some president). If we are educated enough to vote wisely, could this plan work?

Chapter 20. Seed Time of Good Habits   *p. 137*

- Discuss the global enlightenment movement as a social force.
- Why is this a crucial time for peace and democracy in the world?
- Talk about all the ways you've played small in the world. What can you do now to become your highest and best self?
- Discuss the logic behind the idea that in our interactive universe, we each are "co-creators" with God. What does this mean to you?
- Discuss the idea in Judaism of *tikkun olam,* the goal of perfecting or repairing the world. Is social activism our moral duty? Why?

Chapter 21. Begin the World Anew   *p. 145*

- Do you agree that humanity needs a new social contract for our global village? What mistakes of the past do we need to avoid?
- Paine wrote in 1776, "We have it in our power to begin the world over again." Explain how and why we have such a power today.
- The author closes the book with an affirmative prayer that brings together all of the central ideas in the book. Identify these key ideas. Talk about their relevance to your life and your community.
- How has reading *Global Sense* changed your ideas and feelings? What can you do today to change the world by changing yourself?

∞

Expanded study guide: http://mediavisionspress.com/globalsense.html

Think of these things, whence you came, where
you are going, and to whom you must account.
                    – BENJAMIN FRANKLIN

Acknowledgements

THIS book culminates decades of work supported by more people than I could ever thank here. As a start, the people and groups below were vital for me forming and voicing the ideas in *Global Sense.*

Special thanks goes to my family, chiefly my mom and elder sister, plus my nieces and nephews and cousins. I bless the family members passing into spirit since the turn of the century—my father. mother, a sister, an aunt and uncle, and a granduncle. I thank the generations back beyond counting for the family traits I inherited.

Five educators deserve select recognition. Susan Henry in the 8th grade of Denver Public Schools revealed the alchemy of language, a transforming discovery. In the Story Workshop at Columbia College of Chicago, John Schultz and Betty Shiflett helped me find my own writer's voice. A decade later, Sister Lydia Peña at Loretto Heights College in Denver helped me put my lifework in focus. Susan Swan Mura at Antioch taught me about keeping agreements.

Helping me get started as a journalist in the 1970s were John Fink at the *Chicago Tribune* and Lois Martin at *The Aurora Sun.* Publishers Patricia Calhoun at *Westword* and Ron Baccagulupo at *The Denver Downtowner* both opened doors for my talents as few others did back on those halcyon days. They've been mentors and friends.

For inspiration to write this book, I thank each of the authors in the bibliography, which barely begins to list all those enlightening me.

The Windstar Foundation of Aspen introduced me to the major global thinkers of our times. Windstar co-founder Thomas Crum and my friends in the Colorado Connections helped me grow as a person. We all miss John Denver and his vision of higher ground.

Also helping my growth, I want to thank Chérie Carter-Scott and Kirk Stathes of Motivation Management Service; Jon Weiss and Abe Wagner of the USA Transactional Analysis Association; Lori Ohlson and People House; Rick Tidrick and friends of The Gathering Place at Willow Springs; the Colorado Men's Network, ManKind Project, all the men in support groups over the years, including John Arthur Neal; Marilyn McGenity and the Mercury Cafe; Pat Wagner and Leif Smith at Pattern Research; libertarians Karl Hess, Dave Nolan; David Atkins, Dwight Filley; progressives at Camp Wellstone, MoveOn.org, KGNU radio; and such heart friends as Bear Baker, Ray Brejcha, Len Chernila, Chris Farrell, G. Seth Harris, Jon Kinsella, JD Longwell, Victoria Mechling, Joe Mahoney, Colleen Murphy, and Jim Vining. A very special thanks goes to Dr. Sharon Coggan for the habit of saying, "thank you." Each of you has helped me progress on the path.

For updating *Common Sense* into *Global Sense*, I have valued help and interest from the Thomas Paine National Historical Association (thomaspaine.org). Media pioneer Dr. Bernard Luskin mentored me like Benjamin Franklin helped Thomas Paine. Jody Hope Strogoff at *Colorado Statesman* acted akin to Paine's publisher Robert Aitken at *Pennsylvania Magazine*. Wes Dye upheld the vision of prosperity for posterity. Laurie Weiss made plain the logic that Tom Paine writing today would use simpler language than in my early drafts. Joan McWilliams read the conflict resolution section. Catherine O'Neill Thorn and Winnie Shows offered copy editing. Marsha Doyenne and Sara Wade Hutman proofread the text. Mark Oatis inspired my cover design. Jill Rothenberg, Kim Long, Judith Briles, and Kenn Amdahl guided my publishing plans. Britton Slagle was my marketing intern. I bless Naviella Lapidot for her shining lifelight and her invitation to voice essential elements of my own life story in the book.

Thom Hartmann, David Wann and Dr. Vandana Shiva graced the book with its Foreword, Preface and Afterword. Bound for Success (bfsbinding.com) made the initial print editions a reality. Joe Sabah provided tools to get on radio talk shows. Quantum Alchemy was the first retailer to offer *Global Sense*. Tattered Cover bookstore opened double doors for BookSense distribution. Ingram's Lightning Source distributed the title worldwide through Amazon and Barnes & Noble, Friesens printed this edition. New Leaf and Mountain Book Company distributes the book. Publishers Marketing Association, the Colorado Independent Publishers Association, Colorado Authors League, and Denver Press Club are valued allies. I'm grateful to everyone.

Finally, most of all, heartfelt thanks go to Thomas Paine himself, with a prayer my work does justice to the love of liberty. – JF

INDEX

Share *Global Sense* with others!

Give the gift of mindful self rule and personal democracy.

VISIT YOUR FAVORITE BOOKSELLER or ORDER HERE

☐ **YES**, I want ___ *Hardcover* copies of *Global Sense* at **$27.00** each.

☐ **YES**, I want ___ *Softcover* copies of *Global Sense* at **$17.76** each.

For shipping inside the U.S., add **$3** per book for delivery in 5-10 days from receipt of order. Outside the U.S., add **$8** per book for delivery in 4-6 weeks, or for delivery within 10 days, visit <http://postcalc.usps.gov/ratecalc> to find rate for Global Priority Mail. (**Colorado** residents, please add 7% sales tax.)

Subtotal for shipping (*plus 7% sales tax if in Colorado*) US $_____

☐ A **check** or **money order** for TOTAL US $ _____ is enclosed.
Orders from outside the U.S. must be accompanied by a postal money order in U.S. Dollars.

– **OR** –

☐ Please **charge** TOTAL US $ _____ to Visa ___ Mastercard ___
Discover/Novus __ Diners Club __ American Express _ __

Card # _____ Exp. Date ____ / ____ Sec. Code _____ *
*The 3-digit *security code* printed on the back of the card is required to prevent identity theft.

PRINT Name on Card: _____

Phone: _____ Email _____

Signature: _____

Ship to Name: _____

Shipping Address: _____

City, State/Province, Nation: _____ Zip _____

Mail this form to: P.O. Box 181238, Denver CO 80218 USA
Make your check or money order payable to "Media Visions."

OR phone in your order to pay by credit/debit card or e-check.
Toll Free: **1-888-887-1776**
To FAX a credit/debit card order, please call first to request the fax number.

OR order securely online by credit/debit card, echeck or PayPal:
http://mediavisionspress.com/globalsense-order.html

Bookstores, Libraries, Colleges, High Schools: Call Your Book Distributor.
Organizations: Call Media Visions Press toll free to discuss special orders.

– PLEASE PHOTOCOPY THIS ORDER FORM –